Anglican/Roman Catholic Dialogue

The Work of the
Preparatory Commission

Anglican/Roman Catholic Dialogue

The Work of the Preparatory Commission

EDITED BY
ALAN C. CLARK
Auxiliary Bishop of Northampton

AND
COLIN DAVEY
Assistant Chaplain,
Archbishop of Canterbury's Counsellors
on Foreign Relations

LONDON

Oxford University Press

NEW YORK TORONTO

1974

Oxford University Press, Ely House, London W.1

GLASGOW NEW YORK TORONTO MELBOURNE WELLINGTON
CAPE TOWN IBADAN NAIROBI DAR ES SALAAM LUSAKA ADDIS ABABA
DELHI BOMBAY CALCUTTA MADRAS KARACHI LAHORE DACCA
KUALA LUMPUR SINGAPORE HONG KONG TOKYO

ISBN 0 19 213425 6

PRINTED AND BOUND IN ENGLAND BY
HAZELL WATSON AND VINEY LTD
AYLESBURY, BUCKS

Contents

1. The Common Declaration by Pope Paul VI and the
   Archbishop of Canterbury in 1966   1

2. An Introduction to the Work of the
   Joint Preparatory Commission
   by THE REVD. COLIN DAVEY   5

3. Why is Anglican/Roman Catholic Dialogue
   Possible Today?
   by BISHOP J. G. M. WILLEBRANDS   26

4. Where Should Dialogue Begin?
   by PROFESSOR EUGENE R. FAIRWEATHER   37

5. To What Extent Can or Should There Be Diversity
   in a United Church? – Freedom and Authority
   by BISHOP J. G. M. WILLEBRANDS   60

6. Unity and Comprehensiveness
   by BISHOP J. R. H. MOORMAN *and*
   PROFESSOR HOWARD E. ROOT   74

7. Unity: An Approach by Stages?
   by BISHOP HENRY R. MCADOO   84

8. Unity: An Approach by Stages?
   by BISHOP B. C. BUTLER, O.S.B.   101

9. The Malta Report   107
   *Report of the Anglican/Roman Catholic Joint
   Preparatory Commission, after meeting at Gazzada
   (9 to 13 January 1967), Huntercombe Manor
   (31 August to 4 September 1967) and Malta (30
   December 1967 to 3 January 1968)*

10. Letter of Cardinal Bea to the Archbishop of
    Canterbury, dated 10 June 1968   116

11. Resolutions and Report of the Lambeth Conference
    1968 on Anglican/Roman Catholic Relations   120

Index   123

I

The Common Declaration
by Pope Paul VI
and the Archbishop of Canterbury

ROME, SAINT PAUL WITHOUT-THE-WALLS,

Thursday 24 March 1966

In this city of Rome, from which Saint Augustine was sent by Saint Gregory to England and there founded the cathedral see of Canterbury, towards which the eyes of all Anglicans now turn as the centre of their Christian Communion, His Holiness Pope Paul VI and His Grace Michael Ramsey, Archbishop of Canterbury, representing the Anglican Communion, have met to exchange fraternal greetings.

At the conclusion of their meeting they give thanks to Almighty God Who by the action of the Holy Spirit has in these latter years created a new atmosphere of Christian fellowship between the Roman Catholic Church and the Churches of the Anglican Communion.

This encounter of the 23 March 1966 marks a new stage in the development of fraternal relations, based upon Christian charity, and of sincere efforts to remove the causes of conflict and to re-establish unity.

In willing obedience to the command of Christ Who bade His disciples love one another, they declare that, with His help, they wish to leave in the hands of the God of mercy all that in the past has been opposed to this precept of charity, and that they make their own the mind of the Apostle which he expressed in these words: 'Forgetting those things which are behind, and reaching forth unto those things which are before, I press towards the mark for the prize of the high calling of God in Christ Jesus' (cf. Phil 3. 13–14).

They affirm their desire that all those Christians who belong to these two Communions may be animated by these same sentiments of respect, esteem and fraternal love, and in order to help these develop to the full, they intend to inaugurate between the Roman Catholic Church and the Anglican Communion a serious dialogue which, founded on the Gospels and on the ancient common traditions, may lead to that unity in truth, for which Christ prayed.

The dialogue should include not only theological matters such as Scripture, Tradition and Liturgy, but also matters of practical difficulty felt on either side. His Holiness the Pope and His Grace the Archbishop of Canterbury are, indeed, aware that serious obstacles stand in the way of a restoration of complete communion of faith and sacramental life; nevertheless, they are of one mind in their determination to promote responsible contacts between their Communions in all those spheres of Church life where collaboration is likely to lead to a greater understanding and a deeper charity, and to strive in common to find solutions for all the great problems that face those who believe in Christ in the world of today.

Through such collaboration, by the Grace of God the Father and in the light of the Holy Spirit, may the prayer of Our Lord Jesus Christ for unity among His disciples be brought nearer to fulfilment, and with progress towards unity may there be a strengthening of peace in the world, the peace that only He can grant Who gives 'the peace that passeth all understanding', together with the blessing of Almighty God, Father, Son and Holy Spirit, that it may abide with all men for ever.

✠Michael Cantuariensis   Paulus PP. VI

Latin Translation

Hac in Urbe Roma, unde a Sancto Gregorio PP. I missus est in Angliam Sanctus Augustinus, conditor Sedis Cantuariensis, quam omnes, qui nunc sunt, Anglicani quasi centrum suae Communionis Christianae habent, Sanctissimus Dominus Paulus PP. VI et Reverendissimus et Honoratissimus Dominus Michael Ramsey, Archiepiscopus Cantuariensis, Communionis Anglicanae gerens personam, inter se convenerunt, ut fraterno animo salutem sibi impertirent.

Cuius congressionis in fine Deo omnipotenti gratias agunt, quod, Spiritu Sancto afflante, per hos annos proxime elapsos novus sensus Christianae fraternitatis inter Ecclesiam Catholicam Romanam et Ecclesias Communionis Anglicanae est exortus.

Eadem congressione, die XXIII mensis Martii anno MCMLXVI habita, novus quidam efficitur gradus pertinens ad progressionem fraternae necessitudinis rationum, in Christiana caritate innixarum, atque sincerorum conatuum, quibus obstacula, perfectam communionem ecclesiasticam impedientia, superentur.

Praecepto igitur Christi Domini obtemperare cupientes, qui discipulis suis mandavit, ut se invicem diligerent, declarant se in sinu Dei miserentissimi, eiusdem ope, ea cuncta deponere, quae huic praecepto caritatis praeteritis temporibus sunt refragata, et ad mentem Apostoli se accommodare, qui dixit: 'Quae quidem retro sunt obliviscens, ad ea vero, quae sunt priora, extendens meipsum, ad destinatum persequor, ad bravium supernal vocationis Dei in Christo Iesu' (cf. Phil. 3. 13–14).

Edicunt se exoptare, ut fideles utriusque Communionis eodem sensu reverentiae, bonae existimationis, amoris fraterni ducantur. Quam mutuam necessitudinem fovere ac provehere volentes proponunt, ut inter Ecclesiam Catholicam Romanam et Communionem Anglicanam sedulo instituantur colloquia, quorum veluti fundamenta sint Evangelium et antiquae Traditiones utrisque communes, quaeque ad illam unitatem pro qua Christus oravit, in veritate perducant.

Colloquia illa non solum argumenta theologica comprehendent veluti Sacram Scripturam, Traditionem, Liturgiam, sed etiam res illas, quae in vitae usu seu praxi ex utraque parte difficultates habent. Paulus PP. VI ac Archiepiscopus Cantuariensis noverunt quidem gravia obstacula, quae impediunt, ne perfecta communio fidei et vitae sacramentalis restituatur; nihilominus consentientes studiose agere constituunt, ut ex utraque Communione alteri alteros cum auctoritate attingant circa ea omnia, ad vitam ecclesialem spectantia, in quibus mutua opera apta sit ad consensionem et caritatem augendam, atque coniti, ut universae illae graves quaestiones solvantur, quae in mundo nostrae aetatis in Christum credentibus occurrunt.

Hac mutua opera, adiuvante Dei Patris gratia et Sancti Spiritus lumine, citius ad effectum deducatur precatio Domini Nostri Iesu Christi, qua pro unitate discipulorum suorum oravit, et hac progressione, quae fit ad unitatem, pax in humana consortione roboretur, quam solum concedere potest is, qui donat pacem, 'quae exsuperat omnem sensum'; haec vero pax una cum Benedictione Dei omnipotentis, Patris et Filii et Spiritus Sancti, cum omnibus hominibus maneat semper.

✠MICHAEL CANTUARIENSIS   PAULUS PP. VI

2

The Anglican/Roman Catholic
Joint Preparatory Commission

INTRODUCTION

THE REVD. COLIN DAVEY

In November 1965 the Anglican observers at the final session of the Second Vatican Council were received in audience by Pope Paul VI prior to their departure from Rome. The Council had made a profound difference to the Roman Catholic Church and its relations with other Churches. Furthermore its Decree on Ecumenism of November 1964 had declared:

Among those [communions separated from the Holy See] in which some catholic traditions and structures continue to exist, the Anglican Communion occupies a special place. (De Ecum. 13)

So this was not simply an occasion for saying farewell, but a time for talking about the next steps to be taken on the path towards unity. Mention was made of the plans for the Archbishop of Canterbury to visit His Holiness the following spring, and of the possibility of setting up a Joint Commission of Anglicans and Roman Catholics to examine the theological and practical obstacles to unity and to seek ways in which they might be overcome. It was hoped that this official meeting between heads of Churches would both symbolize and signify the opening of a new era in Anglican/Roman Catholic relations. In such a changed climate serious dialogue would also be possible after four centuries of separation and hostility.

The Archbishop of Canterbury was the Pope's guest from 22 to 24 March 1966, and was housed in the Venerable English College. At their meeting in the Sistine Chapel on 23 March the Archbishop spoke of the 'formidable difficulties of doctrine' on the road to unity and of the 'difficult practical matters about which the consciences and feelings of Christian people can be hurt'. He then voiced the hope 'that there may be increasing dialogue between theologians, Roman Catholic and Anglican, and of other traditions, so as to explore together the divine revelation'. He also stressed that such matters must 'be discussed together in patience and charity'. And he added: 'it is only as the world sees us Christians growing visibly in unity that it will accept through us the divine message of Peace'. In his reply His Holiness spoke of 'the historical value of this hour. It appears to us great, almost dramatic, and fortunate, if we think of the long and sorrowful story which it intends to bring to an end, and of the new developments which this hour can inaugurate in the relations between Rome and Canterbury – from now on, friendship must inspire and guide them.'

The following day the Pope and the Archbishop took part in an act of common worship in the Basilica of St. Paul-Without-the-Walls. At its conclusion they made a Common Declaration,[1] in which they announced their intention 'to inaugurate between the Roman Catholic Church and the Anglican Communion a serious dialogue which, founded on the Gospels and on the ancient common traditions, may lead to that unity in truth, for which Christ prayed'. They spoke of 'forgetting those things which are behind, and reaching forth unto those things which are before', and of their 'determination to promote responsible contacts between their Communions in all those spheres of Church life where collaboration is likely to lead to a greater understanding and a deeper charity, and to strive in common to find solutions for all the great problems that face those who believe in Christ in the world of today'.

The Common Declaration announced the opening of the dialogue between Anglicans and Roman Catholics, and laid down guide-lines for those who would take part in it. In the months following the Archbishop of Canterbury's visit to Rome the necessary practical arrangements were made to set up what came to be called the Anglican/Roman Catholic Joint Preparatory Commission.

1. Full Text on pages 1–4.

In May 1966 Bishop (now Cardinal) Willebrands of the Vatican Secretariat for Promoting Christian Unity called on the Archbishop of Canterbury. It was agreed that a Joint Preparatory Commission should be appointed by the Vatican and the Archbishop of Canterbury, after consultation respectively with the Roman Catholic National Hierarchies and the Metropolitans of the Anglican Communion. There would be eight or nine members on each side, from America, Africa, Asia, as well as from Great Britain and the rest of Europe. Each side should have its secretaries and there could be an observer from the World Council of Churches. The aim of the Commission would be to draw up a programme and establish priorities in the theological dialogue, as well as considering matters of practical ecclesiastical co-operation. It would only be after this necessary preparatory work had been done that a further Commission could be set up to engage in the dialogue proper. It was also agreed that a separate special Sub-Commission of four Anglican and four Roman Catholic experts should deal with the question of Mixed Marriages.

In October 1966 Bishop Ralph Dean, the Anglican Executive Officer, the Bishop of Ripon (Dr. J. R. H. Moorman), Canon J. R. Satterthwaite, Canon J. Findlow, and others met at the Vatican Secretariat for Promoting Christian Unity with Bishop Willebrands and his colleagues, Fr. Jerome Hamer and Canon William Purdy, to finalize plans for the first meeting of the Joint Preparatory Commission. It was agreed that two papers should be read on each side, in order to open up discussion, and the following titles were suggested:

(a) Why is Anglican/Roman Catholic dialogue possible today?

(b) Where should Anglican/Roman Catholic dialogue begin, and what are the principal theological points requiring discussion?

It was thought that the work of this Preparatory Commission could be completed in two or three sessions and that the Report it would draw up should be made direct to His Holiness Pope Paul and His Grace the Archbishop of Canterbury. It was agreed that the first meeting would take place from 9 to 13 January 1967. The place eventually chosen was Gazzada near Milan.

On 4 November 1966 the names of the delegates appointed to the Joint Preparatory Commission were published; they were as follows (together with the positions then held):

Anglican Delegates

The Bishop of Ripon (the Rt. Revd. J. R. H. Moorman)	Senior Anglican observer at Second Vatican Council; member of the Archbishop of Canterbury's Commission on Roman Catholic Relations; chairman of the Anglican delegates.
The Revd. Canon James Atkinson	Lecturer in Theology, Hull University.
The Revd. Canon Eric Kemp	Lecturer in Theology and Medieval History, Exeter College, Oxford; University Lecturer in Canon Law.
The Revd. Professor Howard Root	Professor of Theology, Southampton University.
The Bishop of Llandaff (the Rt. Revd. W. G. H. Simon)	Former Warden, St. Michael's College, Llandaff.
The Revd. Dr. Massey H. Shepherd, Jnr.	Professor of Liturgics, Church Divinity School of the Pacific, California.
The Revd. Professor Eugene R. Fairweather	Professor of Dogmatic Theology, Trinity College, Toronto.
The Bishop of Colombo (the Rt. Revd. C. H. W. de Soysa)	Formerly Principal of the Divinity School, Colombo, Ceylon.
The Bishop of Pretoria (the Rt. Revd. E. G. Knapp-Fisher)	Formerly Principal of Cuddesdon Theological College, Oxford.

Secretaries:

The Revd. Canon John Findlow	Archbishop of Canterbury's representative at the Vatican; Associate Secretary of the Archbishop of Canterbury's Commission on Roman Catholic Relations.
The Revd. Canon John R. Satterthwaite	General Secretary of the Church of England Council on Foreign Relations and the Archbishop of Canterbury's Commission on Roman Catholic Relations.

Roman Catholic Delegates

The Rt. Revd. Charles H. Helmsing, Bishop of Kansas City, St. Joseph	Chairman of the United States Roman Catholic Bishops' Commission for relations with the Protestant Episcopal Church.
The Rt. Revd. William Gomes, Titular Bishop of Porlais, Auxiliary to the Archbishop of Bombay	Co-Chairman of the Ecumenical Commission of the Roman Catholic Episcopal Conference of India.
The Rt. Revd. Langton D. Fox	Titular Bishop of Maura and Auxiliary to the Bishop of Menevia, Wales.
The Revd. Louis Bouyer	Priest of the Oratory; French ecumenist; author of many books on ecumenical and liturgical themes.
The Revd. George Tavard	Assumptionist. Professor and head of the Department of Theology at Mount Mercy College, Pittsburg; member of the Roman Catholic Bishops' Commission for relations with the Protestant Episcopal Church in the United States of America; Consultor to the Secretariat for Christian Unity; author of several works on ecumenical themes.
The Revd. Charles Davis	Professor of Theology at the Heythrop College; editor of *The Clergy Review*; author of several books on theological themes.
The Revd. John Keating	Secretary of the English section of the Canadian Roman Catholic Bishops' Commission on Ecumenism.
The Revd. Adrian Hastings	Professor at Kipalapala Seminary, Tabora, Tanzania, and in charge of further education for the East African clergy; author of several ecclesiastical works.
The Rt. Revd. Mgr. J. G. M. Willebrands, Titular Bishop of Mauriana	Secretary of the Secretariat for Promoting Christian Unity, Vatican City.

Secretary:

The Very Revd. Canon W. A. Purdy	Secretariat for Promoting Christian Unity.

There was one subsequent change in the membership. On 21 December Professor Charles Davis announced his decision to leave the Roman Catholic Church. He was replaced by the Revd. Michael Richards of St. Edmund's College, Ware.

Gazzada: 9 to 13 January 1967

On Monday 9 January, the members of the Joint Preparatory Commission assembled at the Conference Centre at the Villa Cagnola, Gazzada, in north Italy. The first evening of their Conference was spent on introductions and practical arrangements. Bishop Helmsing and Bishop Moorman were appointed as Co-Chairmen. The Revd. Paul Verghese was welcomed as the World Council of Churches' Observer.

Tuesday 10 January was devoted to the reading and discussion of three of the four prepared papers. The Commission's task was to arrive at a common statement about the opportuneness, methods, scope, and subject-matter of theological dialogue between the two Communions. The papers by Bishop Moorman and Bishop Willebrands on 'Why is dialogue now possible?' and by Professor Fairweather and Fr. Richards on 'Where should Dialogue begin?', were designed to get the Commission started on this work.

Bishop Moorman gave three reasons why he thought Dialogue was now possible: (1) because we have gone on long enough in our separate compartments; (2) because the Roman attitude towards the problem of Christian Unity has changed so much in the last five years; (3) because many Anglicans have now become interested in the possibility of union with Rome. Bishop Willebrands [2] contrasted the situation in the 1920's with the situation today, and emphasized the differences that were due to the Biblical, Liturgical, and social renewal in the Roman Catholic Church. In the discussion that followed a good deal of time was devoted to the question of how far Anglican plans and schemes for union with the Reformed Churches might affect any hope of union with the Church of Rome. The Commission recognized the need to look at the ecumenical situation as a whole as well as to do justice to the evangelical tradition within Anglicanism.

2. See below, pages 26–36.

Professor Fairweather prefaced his extensive survey[3] of the cardinal issues to be considered in the dialogue with a reminder that 'true ecumenical dialogue demands commitment to the renewal of our own ecclesiastical life . . . a critical eye on our own past and present realization of the Gospel'. There should then be a search, not for some 'minimal agreement' but for the 'crucial Christian truth our formularies are designed to express'. He came to the conclusion that the 'key issues' could be reduced to two: 'The Authority of Christian Doctrine' and 'The Nature of the Gospel'. A lively discussion of the nature of comprehensiveness followed and the importance of seeking agreement on moral witness and in liturgical renewal was underlined.

The next morning, Wednesday 11 January, Fr. Michael Richards read his paper and raised the question: 'Where should dialogue *lead*?' To an *enlarged* Church, he answered, numerically, theologically, devotionally. He felt that four elements in the doctrine of the Church needed to be considered:

(1) *The Church as Communion* – with special reference to Liturgy, the Eucharist, the universal priesthood of all who are 'in Christ', the place of the Blessed Virgin Mary in the economy of salvation, and the relation between Law and Love.

(2) *The Church's Witness to Christ* – introducing problems of Scripture and Tradition, of the Teaching authority of the Church, of a man's personal faith in relation to the rules of the Church.

(3) *The Pastoral Office of the Church* – dealing with the whole apostolic mission, episcopacy, unity and uniformity, the place of the laity in the Church, problems of Church and State, of freedom of conscience, and of education.

(4) *The Uniqueness of the Church* – with special reference to the Roman Catholic claim to be the one and only true Church.

The discussion which followed led the members of the Commission to consider how best to continue their work. They appointed two sub-committees which met on the Wednesday

3. See below, pages 37–59.

evening, one to look at the theological issues and one to draft practical recommendations for the approval of the respective authorities. The first, under Bishop Langton Fox's chairmanship, recommended that at the Commission's next meeting there should be papers on seven subjects. It was agreed that one member should be invited to write and another to open the discussion on these as follows:

1. *What is the Word?*
   Paper by: Father Tavard
   To open discussion: Bishop Simon.
2. *How is the Word received by man?*
   Paper by: Canon Atkinson
   To open discussion: Father Hastings
3. *How does the Word call the Church into being?*
   Paper by: Professor Fairweather
   To open discussion: Father Keating
4. *How does the Church proclaim the Word?*
   Paper by: Father Richards
   To open discussion: Bishop Knapp-Fisher
5. *What should be the minimum structure and essential life of the local church?*
   Paper by: Canon Kemp
   To open discussion: Bishop Fox
6. *How do local Churches form the unity of the Universal Church?*
   Paper by: Father Bouyer
   To open discussion: Dr. Shepherd
7. *To what extent can or should there be diversity in a United Church? – Freedom and Authority*
   Papers by: a. Bishop Willebrands
                        b. Bishop Moorman and Professor Root

It was also agreed that the papers should be made available to all members of the Commission well in advance of the meeting. It was felt that it might be fruitful to focus attention on 'the Word of God' and 'the Church'. By starting with these fundamental points of faith, rather than their instruments – Scripture and Tradition – it was hoped that a sufficient basis of agreement could be built from which to set out to tackle the more problematic and divisive issues.

The sub-committee on practical issues, under Bishop Glyn Simon's chairmanship, recommended, as a matter of urgency, the setting-up of a Joint Commission on the theology of marriage and its relation to the problem of mixed marriages. It also drafted a number of practical recommendations about Anglican/Roman Catholic co-operation which were discussed at length by the whole Commission and were eventually approved for submission to the Pope and to the Archbishop of Canterbury in the following form:

(1) That the Bishops of both Churches should meet more often both socially and for discussion of problems which they have in common.

(2) That the clergy of both Churches should meet, for example in deanery chapters, for the discovering and study of their common heritage and responsibility in Christ.

(3) The formation of local groups of clergy and laity together meeting for prayer, for common study of the Bible and of each other's beliefs and ways of worship, and for Christian witness in social, charitable and educational fields, and any other areas where common action seems possible.

(4) The fostering of oecumenical co-operation at universities and colleges, for Christian witness and service, with the support of the respective chaplains.

(5) The furtherance of Christian unity and mission by the joint use of churches and ancillary buildings wherever possible.

(6) To stress the urgent need to work for common texts in those prayers and formulae which are in use in both Churches.

(7) To urge a greater measure of collaboration in seminary and theological college training and in faculties and departments of theology in universities.

These were eventually further revised and extended to form the practical recommendations in Section II of the Malta Report.[4]

A Press Release was drawn up on Thursday, 12 January. It began by stating that 'After four hundred years of separation between the Roman Catholic and Anglican Churches, official

4. See below, pages 110–11.

representatives from both have taken the first steps towards restoring full unity.' It listed the members of the Commission and the subjects that had been discussed, and referred to the practical recommendations being made. It concluded:

The Conference was held in an atmosphere of daily prayer together; and each delegation, having celebrated the Eucharist according to its own rite, attended the rite of the other. In beginning this new stage in Anglican/Roman Catholic relations, the Commission is humbly grateful for the sense of urgency and Divine guidance throughout the Conference.

It should be added that the atmosphere of the meeting was extremely cordial, that each morning session began with Bible reading and prayer, and that each day ended with a short act of common worship in the chapel. One member wrote afterwards of 'the sense of the movement of the Holy Spirit in the meeting, and the desire to convey this to Christians at large, so anxiously looking for signs of reconciliation among the Churches'. And he concluded: 'Perhaps the chief memory of the meeting is that here was not a leisurely approach to academic dialogue, but a dynamic meeting of very earnest and determined men bent upon healing wounds that had festered for too long'.

The Gazzada Conference ended on the Friday morning, 13 January. The Joint Preparatory Commission planned to meet again at the end of August in England, with a slightly enlarged membership, partly to enable the Anglicans to include a representative of the Liberal Evangelical school of thought.

Huntercombe: 30 August to 4 September 1967

On Wednesday 30 August the Anglican/Roman Catholic Joint Preparatory Commission began its second meeting, this time in England. The place chosen was Huntercombe Manor, a Conference Centre in Buckinghamshire, with a fine fourteenth-century medieval hall in which to meet. Four new members joined the Commission at Huntercombe: two Anglicans, the Revd. Professor Albert T. Mollegen, of Virginia Theological Seminary, a liberal Evangelical from the Episcopal Church of the U.S.A., and the Rt. Revd. H. R. McAdoo, Bishop of Ossory, Ferns and Leighlin, of the Church of Ireland; and two

Roman Catholics, the Rt. Revd. Christopher Butler, O.S.B., formerly Abbot of Downside and now an auxiliary Bishop of Westminster, and Fr. Camillus Hay, O.F.M., from Australia. The Revd. Dr. Harding Meyer, a staff member of the Lutheran World Federation, was present as the Observer from the World Council of Churches.

The task of the Commission was to 'draw up a programme and establish priorities in the theological dialogue, as well as considering matters of practical ecclesiastical co-operation'. Its method was through discussion to see what emerged as the most important issues for Anglicans and Roman Catholics. It would remain to be seen, however, whether this would produce positive results. The Commission were very conscious that they were searching all the time for the best way forward. With this in mind they appointed a sub-commission, chaired by Bishop Butler, to review the progress of the conference as it occurred and to report at the end with proposals on how to proceed at the Commission's next meeting.

Thursday 31 August was devoted to discussion of the papers prepared and circulated in advance on 'The Word of God'. In his paper 'What is the Word?' Fr. George Tavard had presented the all-inclusive Biblical understanding of the Word of God as active, powerful, and creative. It is also a 'word of judgment', he added, in the light of which all theologies must be examined and criticized. The Church is servant, not mistress, of the Word, recipient, not exponent, of the Word, though she witnesses to the Word. Word and Scripture are not identical. Nor should we identify too closely how and by whom the Word is authoritatively interpreted. The Counter-Reformation wrongly thought of the Word as spoken *by* rather than *to* the Church. The Second Vatican Council has begun to restore the proper balance of the biblical picture.

Bishop Simon opened the discussion of this paper which centred on the authority of the New Testament and the authority of the individual or the Church to interpret Scripture. Roman Catholic speakers added that the Church is the guardian as well as the recipient of the Word.

'How is the Word received by man?' Through the Scriptures, through the Church, and through human experience, Canon James Atkinson had written. He emphasized the

Reformers' view that only the converted, through the internal testimony of the Holy Spirit, can read God's Word aright. He added that their understanding of the sufficiency of Scripture means that the Roman Catholic Church's proclamation of, for instance, the dogma of the Assumption of the Blessed Virgin Mary as *de fide* was 'unwarrantable, unnecessary, and irreligious'. Scripture itself, not the Church or current scholarship, is the final arbiter in any perplexity, and a self-authenticating authority beyond conscience, reason, or secular power. God speaks to man also through the Church, the Servant of the Word, in its preaching, prayer, and pastoral care. (The protest of the Reformers, he added, was that the Roman Church had ceased to proclaim the Word.) The wrath of God, the activity of conscience, the voice of concerned admonition: these are three ways in which God speaks to man through his human experience.

Fr. Adrian Hastings spoke to this and began with a warning against the danger of identifying ourselves with the people on one side or the other at the time of the Reformation. He urged members to build bridges, not to perpetuate divisions. At the close of the discussion which followed Bishop Willebrands did just this. He pointed out that the Commission had been trying to answer the question, 'What is authoritative and what is the place and function of authority in the Church?' The latter, he suggested, is to discern what the Holy Spirit is saying to the Churches. It follows, he added, that we shall move forward if together we seek to discover what is authentically Christian both in the intentions of the Reformers and in the Roman Catholic Church. He was ready, he concluded, to do penance for all the legalism in the latter and hoped that this would help towards the restoration of full relations between us.

Professor Eugene Fairweather's paper on 'How the Word of God creates and sustains the Church' described God's Word to man as a redemptive self-disclosure. The Church is created, renewed, and sustained by the Holy Spirit in sacramental action and verbal proclamation. This leads to the complex questions of Tradition, Scripture, and Magisterium, for it is 'essential that the Sacraments and the Word by which Christ is perpetually presented to his Church should be true to what they represent'.

Fr. John Keating introduced a short discussion of this, which set the Commission talking about the nature and shape of the visible Church and its ministry, including the Papacy. At this point it was felt useful to turn to the paper by Fr. Michael Richards on 'How does the Church proclaim the Word?'

This began with the problem of how to 'maintain the supremacy of the Word of God over the Church, while at the same time according to the Church a permanent responsibility for watching over and proclaiming the Word?' Fr. Richards stated that a fundamental difference between Anglicans and Roman Catholics was over the notion that the Church's proclamation of the Word is unfailingly guaranteed by God. He argued in favour of a greater deference to the Church, to what is proclaimed and taught by Popes and Councils and Bishops and by priests and lay people. For the whole Church 'has received the promise of freedom from error in Faith, in order that the mission of the whole Church may be truly carried out'. Theological speculation, however, is not given the same guarantee. The voice of the Spirit, he concluded, is heard precisely in the coincidence and interplay between the individual and the community of the Church.

In opening discussion of this, Bishop Knapp-Fisher contrasted the authority of the whole and undivided Church with that of 'any particular part of a still divided Church'. The traditional Anglican attitude, he said, is that authority may be strong and persuasive but, in a divided Church, never absolute or infallible or coercive. The debate which followed was mostly about 'apostolic succession', in doctrine, in the college of bishops, in the episcopal or presbyteral ministry. Professor Root called for a re-examination of the concept of validity. Fr. Hastings felt that a minimum statement on the ministry could be drawn up that would be acceptable to both sides. Bishop Moorman, in closing, pointed to the crucial issue between Roman Catholics and Anglicans of whether or not the Church is still thought of as undivided – whether schism is within or from the Church.

On Friday 1 September the papers on the Church were discussed. Canon Eric Kemp had answered the question, 'What should be the minimum structure and essential life of the local Church?' The diocese, he emphasized, is the fundamental

unit of church organization, under its Father-in-God, the
Bishop, who duly authorizes ministers to preach the Word of
God and administer the sacraments in the congregation of the
baptized. The Bishop is the centre of unity for the diversity
of Christians in his diocese. Bishop, clergy, and laity, however,
co-operate in church government, for ultimate authority lies
with the whole body, and the 'sharp distinction between
ecclesia docens and *ecclesia discens* is not congenial to Anglicans'. He concluded by drawing attention to a major difference
of emphasis between Roman Catholics and Anglicans over the
rights and independence of the local church: 'most Anglicans
would have no difficulty in giving to the Papacy the kind of
appellate jurisdiction assigned to it by the Council of Sardica.
Where they would find difficulty is in being asked to acknowledge that the Pope has by divine commission the right to
intervene with ordinary authority in the affairs of local churches, to restrict their bishops in their pastoral office, or to sup-
press local hierarchies'. In speaking to this paper Bishop
Langton Fox contrasted the way in which Canon Kemp saw
the bishop primarily as pastor of the local Church and his own
view of him 'first as a member of the episcopal college succeeding the apostolic college in the ministry of teaching, jurisdiction, and order'. He added that for a Roman Catholic ultimate
authority lay with the episcopal college, though acceptance
of its teaching by the whole body was necessary. In conclusion
he suggested that it might be fruitful to consider together what
sort of primacy the Church needs for its unity and indefectibility.

Considerable discussion followed about the functions of
bishops and the theology of the local church. Fr. Camillus Hay
felt an inconsistency between this latter and the Roman Catholic concept of jurisdiction, while Bishop Butler was encouraged
to find that differences of opinion on these issues were between
members of both Churches rather than along denominational
lines.

Fr. Louis Bouyer's paper was entitled 'The Papal Supremacy in relation to the Unity and Unicity of the Church'.
Like Canon Kemp, he began with the local church as the basic
manifestation of the Church of Christ. He emphasized, however, that the local bishop was not simply the centre of local

unity, but the link of unity with other Churches, because of his membership of the college of bishops, the successors of the Twelve. The Bishop of Rome, the successor of Peter, has a special responsibility to promote the unity of the Churches. Provided that this responsibility is seen as *ministerium* not as *dominium*, he will support, not diminish, the power of the bishops, and there will be no opposition between papal and conciliar church government. Fr. Bouyer stressed that Papal definitions enjoyed the same infallibility as pertains to the Church as a whole. The Pope is protected by Divine Providence from leading the Church into error. He added that the Pope's universal jurisdiction means that he can intervene 'whenever and wherever it is needed for the sake of the Unity of the whole and of the different parts as parts of the whole'. This right does not however mean that he will always act rightly. Fr. Bouyer ended his paper by answering the question, 'What do we mean when we say that the Catholic Church is the one true Church, and her alone?' 'The one true Church', he wrote, 'is that in which there is the unity of the true faith and of the true life in love springing from the authentic sacraments of the true faith'. The Pope, and the episcopal body in communion with him, is the supreme human instrument for the maintenance of that unity, so that communion with him is a token that a local Church is part of the one true Church. The Orthodox Churches of the East, however, 'where the substance of the Catholic faith and sacraments is preserved' are part of the true Church, though in the abnormal situation of not being in communion with the Pope. Fr. Bouyer rejected the description of this situation as schism within the Church. He felt, however, that the Anglican and Protestant Churches were in real schism from the Church. Nevertheless, their Christian life and love were often a reproach to the members of the one true Church, and a challenge to penitence and collective reformation. He longed for their 'reintegration to the one true Church, which, even without their knowing it, remains their native home'.

The discussion of this paper was introduced by Professor Massey Shepherd with a paper of his own which asked whether primacy was a matter of faith or of constitutional law, and argued that the historical supports of authority must be as

satisfactory as possible. The debate which followed was much
concerned with the functioning of the Papacy in the past, but
Bishop Helmsing reminded the Commission that they ought
also to ask 'How is collegiality going to develop and work in
the renewed Roman Catholic Church?' Fr. Hastings asked for
a closer analysis of what is meant by describing the See of Peter
as an 'organ of unity'. Bishop Willebrands felt that in our
developing situation further dialogue was necessary in order
to discover both how we *can* live together and also the form in
which the papacy can be exercised, rather than ask at this
stage 'what is the essential doctrine which we have to accept
about the papacy?'

After further discussion of the papacy, Bishop Moorman
invited Bishop Willebrands to introduce his paper 'To what
extent can or should there be diversity in a united Church?'[5]
This was sub-titled 'Freedom and Authority' and in presenting
it the author emphasized 'the growth and continuity of the
Church, and also freedom for God's intervention in that continuity'. 'Authority', he added, 'is as much submitted to liberty
as liberty has to be guided by authority, and yet must not
diminish that liberty.' He spoke also of the idea of the local
Church, and the basis given in the Second Vatican Council
for a new development of it, 'with all the problems that it will
cause for the papacy and central authority'. 'It is good', he
said, 'that those problems will arise, that there will be greater
diversity within our Church, otherwise we will not be able to
go ahead to history'.

In the discussion which followed Bishop McAdoo spoke of
the distinction in Anglican theology between fundamentals
of the faith and 'secondary truths'. He referred to the idea of
a 'hierarchy of truths' in Vatican II's Decree on Ecumenism
and of the possibility of agreement on the fundamentals of the
faith, along the lines of the Bonn Agreement of 1931 between
the Church of England and the Old Catholics, which included
the words 'each believes the other to hold all the essentials of
the Christian faith'. Bishop Butler then spoke of degrees of
unity in faith and also of degrees in the achievement of unity
and communion.

The final paper, prepared by Bishop Moorman and Profes-

5. See below, pages 60–73.

sor Root, entitled 'Unity and Comprehensiveness'[6] was then presented. It began with the Anglican view that 'comprehensiveness is a necessary quality in any Church which pretends to catholicity', but it also pointed to the proper place given to diversity by the Roman Catholic Church, particularly in the documents of the Second Vatican Council. Diversity raises the problems of continuity in faith and of the need for some centre and focus of authority and unity. Anglican/Roman Catholic dialogue would also need to discuss the limits of diversity in dogma and devotion, and on moral questions.

The two delegations met separately after dinner to review progress, formulate suggestions for discussion during Saturday and Sunday, and to help prepare the agenda for the third meeting of the Commission.

Saturday 2 September began with the presentation of the points made by the two groups, and a general discussion of the feasibility of progressing towards unity by stages. It was agreed that a sub-commission should prepare a document to work on at the next meeting, which could become 'a plan to put forward for the Churches to consider' to be submitted to the Pope and the Archbishop of Canterbury and available also for the Lambeth Conference of July 1968. This was then referred to the committee under Bishop Butler to work out more fully.

The remainder of Saturday was then devoted to a discussion of the Anglican/Methodist Conversations in England and a further consideration of the paper by Fr. Bouyer and the question of schism within the Church.

On Sunday morning, 3 September, Bishop Butler presented his committee's recommendations. These were that the proposed document should begin with a general introduction underlining the present unprecedented situation of a world convergence towards Christian unity and the need for unprecedented, but theologically justified, steps to be taken to meet it. It would consider the feasibility of an officially authorized progress towards unity by stages. It would suggest that 'neither side should require from the other, as a condition of very much greater unity, a positive acceptance as of faith of every article in one's own creed'. Conditions of intercommunion might then be spelt out, and a number of practical

6. See below, pages 74–83.

points added, setting out ways of extending Anglican/Roman Catholic co-operation.

It was agreed that Bishop Butler and Bishop McAdoo with the help of Fr. Richards and Professor Root, would draw up this draft document for consideration at the Commission's third meeting at the end of the year.

Canon Purdy and Canon Findlow were asked to consider whether the question of Anglican Orders should be re-opened at this stage, and if so, how it should be approached.

A Press Release was approved, which pointed out that the discussion of the papers had thrown 'into relief certain points of crucial importance, e.g. the authority to interpret Holy Scripture, Episcopacy, Papal Primacy and Infallibility, dogmatic definitions about the Blessed Virgin Mary, Anglican Orders, and the problems connected with intercommunion'. It 'welcomed the appointment of a Joint Commission on the theology of marriage and its application to mixed marriages, which was urgently recommended at Gazzada'. It expressed encouragement at the issuing of the first part of the Directory on Ecumenism by the Vatican Secretariat for Promoting Christian Unity. It endorsed the practical recommendations made in the Directory for the joint use of church buildings and for the use of common liturgical texts. It added that there was a need for a 'greater measure of collaboration in education for the Sacred Ministry and in faculties and departments of theology in universities', for the Commission felt that the education of the laity in the demands and responsibilities of Christian unity depends upon the ecumenical training of the clergy.

The following words by a member of the Commission describe the sense of growing together experienced at Huntercombe:

As at Gazzada, it was pre-eminently in morning and evening worship together that Anglicans and Roman Catholics found and recognized one another as brethren in Christ, more united than separated; though sharing in the Eucharistic celebrations of the respective Churches still has, by mutual consent, to fall short of full intercommunion. This was experienced at once as a deprivation due to division and as the most urgent incentive to overcome it. All were conscious all the time of the help of the Holy Spirit given not least through the quantity and quality of prayer being offered on both sides throughout the world. At Huntercombe, fellowship at this level was deepened as well as mutual sympathy and friendship. This is one of the most important results, intangible though it may be, and difficult as it is to express in the churches represented.

Malta: *30 December 1967 to 3 January 1968*

The Anglican/Roman Catholic Joint Preparatory Commission held its third and final meeting at a newly built Jesuit conference centre in Malta. This was the retreat house of Mount St. Joseph, Mosta, which is situated on a hill which overlooks St. Paul's Bay, where the Apostle was shipwrecked. It was hoped that a similar fate would not befall the Commission! The membership at Malta was the same as at Huntercombe, except that Bishop Simon and Dr. Harding Meyer, the World Council of Churches' Observer, were unfortunately unable to be present.

Bishop McAdoo and Bishop Butler had each prepared a paper entitled 'Unity: An Approach by Stages'.[7] They had also compiled together a 'suggested outline for a Joint Draft Document'. These, together with the report by Canon Findlow and Canon Purdy which recommended that the question of Anglican orders should be approached not in isolation but in the context of the doctrine of the Church, sacraments, and ministry, formed the basis of the discussions and work at Malta. This consisted of the preparation, paragraph by paragraph, of the Commission's report and recommendations, which were finally agreed unanimously and came to be known as 'The Malta Report'.[8]

The Press Release issued at the conclusion of the meeting spoke first of the progress of the Commission's work:

The task at Gazzada was to survey the field and identify the themes on which dialogue might best centre. As a result, at Huntercombe we concentrated our attention on the theme of revelation and its embodiment in the life of the Church. Concurrently at both meetings a sense of the pressure of the time forced us to attend to practical matters and make certain recommendations.

It was exciting to find at the end of this that we felt the need and saw the possibility of plotting some course towards unity. The scheme adopted for our third meeting was an attempt to respond to this vision.

7. See below, pages 84–100 and 101–6.   8. See below, pages 107–15.

The Report of the Commission was to be submitted immediately to Pope Paul VI and the Archbishop of Canterbury.

We believe [the Press Release continued] that in the perspective of post-Reformation history this report stands out, as containing the first formal joint statement ever made of the faith we rejoice to share. A just estimate of the value and extent of this gives us confidence in moving forward on to more difficult ground, that of confronting seriously the differences that keep us apart.

We have made recommendations in this regard both for dialogue and for practical measures for growing together, but we feel that this moving forward by tackling difficulties will not prosper unless we widely share our experiences and learn from each other at every level of life in our Communions.

We make these recommendations, aimed at deepening and enriching our common life in Christ, because we know that only the shared experience of renewal can show what further steps we must take. But it is clear now that, whatever these further steps may turn out to be, scholars on both sides should already be engaged in serious joint study of such difficulties as those arising out of the constitution and teaching office of the Church, the place of Mary in the faith and devotion of the Church, and ministry.

The encouragement they felt at what had been achieved is shown in their closing words:

As the preparatory task assigned to us is completed, we thank God for having guided and strengthened our efforts and blessed us with many personal insights, the fruit of much warm, human sympathy and friendship. In three meetings we have had only a single absentee, and that unavoidable. Nothing could have been stronger than our own experience in the discussions to convince us of the value of dialogue and of growing together and of the vital need to extend these to every place where our Communions are in contact.

Bishop William Gomes of Poona wrote later:

When I look back at the meetings of Gazzada and Huntercombe I realize how both these played a decisive role in paving the way for the historic meeting at Malta. To my mind the common denominator in all these meetings was the warmth of Christian fellowship coupled with frank and outspoken dialogue. We prayed in common each day, and we are most grateful to the people of Malta for spending a Night Vigil in prayer for the success of these unity talks. In the final analysis, it is the Holy Spirit that must guide our two Communions, slowly but surely, to the ultimate goal of Christian Unity.

After submission of the Malta Report to the Pope and the Archbishop of Canterbury, it was sent in confidence to the Metropolitans of the Anglican Communion for comment. In June 1968 Cardinal Bea wrote to the Archbishop of Canterbury[9] to convey the Pope's gratitude for the work of the Joint Preparatory Commission and to express agreement that an Anglican/Roman Catholic 'Permanent Joint Commission' should be set up to carry out the dialogue between the two Churches on the general lines laid down in the Malta Report. Permission was not given for the publication of the Report, but it was agreed that it could be communicated to the bishops, consultants, and observers at the Lambeth Conference, which met in July–August 1968.

The Anglican response to the Malta Report is contained in Resolutions 52, 53, and 54 of the Lambeth Conference. These welcomed the proposals made in the Section Report on Anglican Relations with the Roman Catholic Church, recommended the setting up of a Permanent Joint Commission, and urged the speedy continuance of the working of the Joint Commission on the Theology of Marriage and its Application to Mixed Marriages.[10]

In November 1968 the Malta Report was leaked to the press and was printed in *The Tablet,* the *Church Times, Herder Correspondence,* and elsewhere.

The 'Permanent Joint Commission' was appointed in 1969 and held its first full meeting at Windsor in January 1970, when it changed its name to the 'Anglican/Roman Catholic International Commission'.

The dialogue continues.

9. See below, pages 116–19.   10. See below, pages 120–2.

3

Why is Anglican/Roman Catholic Dialogue Possible Today?

A PAPER READ AT GAZZADA, 10 JANUARY 1967

BISHOP J. G. M. WILLEBRANDS

When this meeting was planned in Rome last October it was agreed that the opening reports, of which this is one, should not be historical discourses in the ordinary sense. They should answer the question 'Why is Anglican/Catholic dialogue possible today?' While recognizing that we do not start from zero, they should follow the spirit of that passage of Philippians quoted in common by Pope and Archbishop at St. Paul's[1]: they should concentrate on the *present* situation, on the opportunity and favourable conditions for dialogue which it offers.

My own suggestion, welcomed then, was that suitable limits for my paper might be set by contrasting the Anglican/Roman situation at the time of *Mortalium Animos* (1928) with that of today. There is no lack of scope for this. But any historical point of departure is arbitrary. The Encyclical *Mortalium Animos* as a papal utterance reflects an historical attitude, and relies on previous utterances. I must briefly mention three:

On 16 September 1864 the Holy Office addressed a letter *Ad Omnes Episcopos Angliae* forbidding Catholic participation in that Association for the Promotion of Christian Unity founded by F. G. Lee and in the periodical *The Union Review* which the Holy Office wrongly assumed to be merely expressing the association's opinions. The Holy Office was wrong too, as was subsequently protested, in assuming that this movement

---

1. 'Forgetting those things which are behind and reaching forward to those things which are before, I press towards the mark for the prize of the high calling of God in Christ Jesus' (cf. Phil. 3. 13–14). (See Common Declaration of the Pope and the Archbishop of Canterbury, pages 1–2 above.)

rested on the so-called Branch Theory; but what I am chiefly interested in here is the language of the Holy Office letter. It reflected the extreme ultramontanism of Manning and the eccentric Talbot. It reflected the fact that the Vatican did not enjoy then, nor for long afterwards, sound information or broadly-based advice on English affairs. In 1919, less than a decade before *Mortalium Animos*, they raised the question at the Holy Office whether the 1864 decree ought to remain in force, and its provisions be extended to all unity meetings organized by non-Catholics. The answer, predictably, was *'affirmative'*. Fifty-five years it seemed had changed nothing. To say that this was so in fact would be unfair to Leo XIII, who may be remembered for other things besides *Apostolicae Curae*. Nevertheless, the same sort of language appears, e.g., in his letter *Ad Anglos*.

Again in 1927, on 8 July, the Holy Office, in anticipation of the Lausanne Faith and Order meeting, August 1927, decided it must stand by its decree of 1919.

Mortalium Animos certainly seemed to put a crown on this monolithic structure. Yet we must remember that it was more a criticism of the Ecumenical Movement as it then existed than an expression of Pius's attitude to separated Christians. This is better expressed in an address given earlier in the same year to the University Catholic Federation:

For reunion it is above all necessary to know one another and to love one another. It is necessary to know one another because it may be said that if the work of reunion has so often failed, these failures have been due in large part to the fact that neither side has known the other. If there have been mutual prejudices, these prejudices must be resolved. The errors and equivocations that exist and are repeated among the separated brethren against the Catholic Church seem incredible. But on the other hand, Catholics too have sometimes been lacking in a just evaluation of their duty or, because of lack of acquaintance, in friendly devotion. Do we know all the precious, good and Christian things that these segments of ancient Catholic truth possess? The separated particles of gold-bearing rock themselves contain gold.

Twenty years separated *Mortalium Animos* from the *Monitum* of the Holy Office of June 1948. This is an eloquent if indirect testimony to the stirrings in Catholic hearts. I quote the first part of it:

Since it appears that in some places, contrary to Canon Law and without permission of the Holy See, joint meetings of Catholics and non-Catholics have been held to discuss matters of faith, all are reminded that Canon 1325 Sec. 3 forbids these meetings without permission to laity, clerics and religious. Much less is it lawful for Catholics to summon or establish such conferences.

The Holy Office can do no more than draw attention to the state of the law. It does not seem then to have grasped that the state of reality might have left the law behind. Again we wonder what was the relation between this Vatican department and its prefect – the Pope. Perhaps the Pope, Pius XII, wondered too. Anyway, the following year the Instruction on Ecumenism, if not a revolutionary document, at least paid the Ecumenical Movement the compliment of a great deal more space and a rather more sympathetic preamble. We may allow further that it represents an advance on anything that had gone before in the way of concrete concessions. Catholic relations with our separated brethren result from complex historical forces in each country, and there may be some recognition of this when the *Instructio* gives bishops some scope in dealing with these relations. If we look forward towards the Second Vatican Council it is even more interesting to see that some initiative is urged on episcopal conferences, but the prevailing impression left by the tone and content of this *Instructio* (which was intended to anticipate the Amsterdam Assembly of the World Council of Churches) is that little is understood of ecumenism as a state of mind, governing without compromising religious thinking and practice. The contrast between the *Instructio* and the Council's decree *Unitatis Redintegratio* is sufficiently obvious. We may now consider what influences converged in the interval to promote ecumenical thinking among Catholics at large.

Biblical Renewal

Forces of renewal were at work. First we must put biblical renewal. As late as 1946 Ronald Knox, a loyal yet candid Catholic, speaking of the Catholic attitude to the Scriptures could say that 'we have a score of good fighting texts at our fingertips, landmarks in the history of controversy. And for the rest the whole treasure house of the gospels is there at our elbow and somehow we never seem to have more than a nodding acquaintance with it.'

Happily, there were already movements afoot to make this criticism, if not out of date, certainly more limited in relevance. The mood and the methods prompted by the Modernist alarm hampered the proper participation of Catholic scholars in the remarkable advance of biblical scholarship between the wars. These were particularly impressive of course in the field of archaeology and related sciences which revolutionized the approach to the Bible. It was not well appreciated in Rome that these advances affected non-Catholic Christian scholars beneficially, making them less influenced by nineteenth-century prejudices. There were contacts between Catholic and Protestant or Jewish biblical scholars: we can remember gratefully that our own Cardinal Bea, when lecturing at the Biblical Institute in Pius XI's time, was invited to take part in an international Biblical Conference, went somewhat diffidently to Pius to ask whether he should go and was told he certainly must. But such examples were still too rare.

In 1943, when the war distracted attention from such a landmark, Pius XII issued his encyclical *Divino Afflante Spiritu*. It celebrated the fiftieth anniversary of Leo XIII's *Providentissimus Deus* but was mainly concerned to emphasize that 'the position of Biblical studies had greatly changed during the past half century'. Excavation (hardly begun in Palestine when Leo wrote), the discovering of papyri and codices, more exact study of the Early Fathers, have given new dimensions and stimulus to biblical study; so have the remarkable advances in ancient languages and philosophy. These aids should support the contemporary scholar in his search for the author's meaning and for theological content. 'The faithful want to know what God has told us in Holy Scripture.' Modern scholarship has deepened our insights into the meaning of inspiration. The interpreter must 'go back in spirit to those remote times' with the help of history, archaeology, ethnology and so on – searching out the ancient writers' proper mode of expression. If today many problems persist, the general effect of this more scholarly approach, says the Pope, has been to restore rather than diminish confidence in the history of the Bible.

The encyclical grew out of a reaction to conservative extravagance in Italy, but that was not its most important aspect. A renewal of scholarly concern with the Bible, of scholarly cooperation with other Christians and with men of all beliefs was in this document finally forcing its way out at the top, so to speak. You all know that it was not the end of obstructionism against biblical scholarship, but it was perhaps the end of a world in which obstructionism could hope to succeed permanently.

Some of you will remember the stirring history of the Constitution *On DivineRevelation* during the days of Vatican II. I shall refer to it again. Here I think of it mainly because of the way it brought about one of the most striking of the many conciliar activities outside the Council aula.

Most of the bishops had studied Scripture at a period when the light shed by *Providentissimus Deus* had been blacked out by the Modernist crisis and not yet restored by *Divino Afflante Spiritu*. To equip themselves for their conciliar function of witnessing to the truth they turned energetically and in great numbers to the experts. It was thus that a majority was created in favour of rejecting the first Schema on Revelation which would have made real debate impossible and which was candidly described in the Council as 'theologically immature', 'unsympathetic to scientific research,' 'incomprehensible to non-Catholics'. At this decisive moment in the Second Vatican Council the Episcopal College recaptured the ancient Catholic tradition of holding sound learning and hard thinking in high honour.

Liturgical Renewal

If *Divino Afflante Spiritu* and the Council utterances in the biblical field seem like revolutionary documents tenaciously resisted in some quarters, Liturgical renewal has had a more serene history; Catholic and other Christian studies have for longer followed parallel ways. Liturgical learning has been enriched by Catholic and non-Catholic scholars alike. In England it was even given permanent form in such societies as the Camden, the Bradshaw, and the Surtees. We should not forget here the recall to the fundamentals of religion prompted by the war. Diekman has written 'it was in army and war prison camps when reduced to the bare essentials of worship, in a personal encounter of priest and lay soldiers stripped of all external props, that the reality of the Liturgy and the meaning of the Church were discovered anew by thousands. To this discovery the pastoral liturgical renewal of the post-war years largely owes its dynamism.' Here too a famous Papal Encyclical, *Mediator Dei*, canalized a strong movement within the Church as a whole, and not least in the mission field. It was a movement, moreover, which was felt throughout the Christian world, and not least in the Anglican Communion.

The vital factor, it has been said, is not the practical details of ritual technique but the spiritual consciousness of our people. The enrichment we are seeking to give them is the re-awakened sense of the assembly of Christians as a basic reality of Christian life.

With the Second Vatican Council's Constitution *On the Liturgy* the liturgical movement in a few weeks ceased to have all the provisional, struggling, minority character associated with the term 'movement', and became firmly incorporated in the Church's life. Regulation of it too became much more broadly based. The conception of the people of God grouped liturgically round its bishop is already prominent in the constitution and points to the *Constitutio De Ecclesia*. The Liturgical Constitution as a conciliar act is an act of collegiality, making provision for acts of collegiality in daily liturgical life. The flexibility of the dispositions for liturgical reform, the responsibilities given to episcopal conferences, also point clearly to the social changes which had so much prompted liturgical reforms, as the reforms themselves constantly reflect the Scriptural renewal already briefly discussed.

Social Movement

Speaking in the Liturgy debate, Bishop Ancel of Lyons urged those Bishops who had no pastoral charge to try to understand the plight of pastors who were faced with situations in which the church was considered moribund and appreciate their longing for a liturgical renewal. Bishops who still enjoyed the security of large docile congregations were asked not to close their eyes and hearts to the needs of those living in de-Christianized areas where the mere pouring in of money would be of little use.

These are the words of a bishop whose repute derives chiefly from his intimate association, maintained through many ups and downs, with the vital social movement in the French Church. Nowhere has the need to recapture the modern masses for Christ been more radically faced. As one of your English university historians has put it, speaking of the period following the denouncing of the Concordat by the Republic in the early years of this century 'a new missionary spirit was awakened among the clergy and the old bureaucratic attitude became less common. In varied ways the Church tackled the problem of keeping a hold on the people.'

Cardinal Verdier and many following in his wake have had the courage to speak of a 'de-Christianized France' and to draw the conclusion that pastoral methods that created this situation are obsolete.

I do not need to stress that there have been similar stirrings in the Anglican Church. It is enough to mention movements and writings associated with the name of William Temple.

Is there a thread that runs through these three kinds of change? It might well be seen as the thread of pure scholarship; the scientific spirit not in the sense of an assumption that material knowledge is the end of all inquiry, or that no method but that of the natural sciences can lead man to truth; but rather in the sense of a meticulous regard for fact, a wholly disinterested effort to understand both past history as it was and present reality as it is. Research as the servant of understanding, not the servant of propaganda or the bolsterer of received opinions.

Such a candid attention to fact in the world of today could not fail to provoke a radical re-examination of accepted ideas. Could the gulf which had been opened between the Church and the world be seriously thought of as unconnected with the way the official Church presented itself to the world? You will remember that when the original schema *De Ecclesia* was presented to the Council it was vigorously attacked on just this ground. It conceived the Body of Christ not as a divine mystery but merely as a legal institution. The Church, said the critics, was not a pyramid of people, priests and pope, so much as the whole people of God, the organic, mystical body. The Hierarchy's primary function was to serve, not to be the object of 'hierarcholatry'.

We must remember that it was the bishops themselves, acting collegially, who sealed the fate of this document, which they saw as travestying the nature of the Church of which they were pastors. A year later a radically revised text was voted by the bishops: they had those months in which to consider the vital question of what the Church is, of how she shall present herself to a world which is not interested in her past triumphs, her complex historic organization, the splendours of her ceremonial or the intricacies of her legal system. They adopted the text by a majority of 2231 votes to 43.

Whatever might be the theological significance of the debate on the collegial status of bishops, the debate itself was the clearest exercise of that status. It was collegial action too that fashioned and voted the final constitution, presenting the Church afresh as 'a sign and instrument of the intimate union of the whole human race with God', making her known in all the richness of her life and attributes, as she reveals herself in the words of Our Lord in the Gospel and in the preaching of the apostles, especially St. Paul. It was within this picture that the constituent elements of the church – episcopate, priesthood, religious, laity and their relations to each other were examined.

In the same context of the People of God the constitution lays the foundation for the Decree *On Ecumenism* by briefly examining the Church's relations with those Christians who do not have full visible union with the Catholic Church. Earlier controversies about 'degrees of membership' are avoided. Emphasis is on positive links – baptism, scripture and so on (*De Eccelesia* 15).

Let us enlarge a little upon one of these positive links. In Chapter VI of the Constitution *On Divine Revelation* which treats of 'Sacred Scripture in the Life of the Church' the Council not only vindicates the rightful place of Scripture 'together with sacred Tradition the Supreme Rule of Faith': it urges what no official document has done for many centuries, that easy access to sacred Scripture should be provided for all the faithful especially in translations from the original texts. I should like to quote the succeeding sentence of the Constitution in full:

and if given the opportunity and the approval of Church authority these translations are produced in cooperation with the separated brethren, all Christians will be able to use them.

This sentence has provided the warrant for a most eventful series of negotiations which have reached a critical stage in Rome during the past week: negotiations by which the Catholic Church may hope to profit by the collaboration 'freely offered' of that very remarkable world wide organization, the United Bible Societies.[2] This chapter of the Constitution goes on to give unstinted encouragement to biblical scholars; to assert that 'the Sacred Page is as it were the Soul of Sacred Theology' and to demand that all the people of God, clergy and laity, shall have the will and the facility to attain a knowledge of Scripture adequate to their state.

In the Constitution on *The Church in the World of Today*, the Council of Bishops insist that they proceed from more deep examination of the mystery of the Church to speak 'not only to the Church's sons and to those who call on the name of Christ but to all men, anxious to explain to all how it understands the presence and function of the church in the world of today'. A horizontal consideration, so to speak, follows a consideration in depth. 'Men must be saved, human society restored' says the Constitution. The two tasks are inseparable. Christian history gives venerable witness to their conjunction. This 'horizontal' consideration is essentially that found in the second chapter of *De Ecclesia* on the People of God:

The Church believes that Christ, who died and rose from the dead for all of us, gives man through His spirit light and strength enough to live up to his high vocation; nor is there any other name under heaven given among men by which we must be saved. She believes that the key, the centre and purpose of all human history is to be found in her Lord and Master. The Church claims that beneath all change there are many things unchanging which have their ultimate foundation in Christ who is the same yesterday and today and forever.

2. Since these words were written at the end of 1966, the collaboration referred to has advanced and spread with remarkable rapidity.

Here surely in a time of uncertainty like ours, a time of rapid change when standards are too easily seen as relative, is a powerful inspiration Christians must have in common. The dignity of the human person, the worth of the human community, the determining of the rightful autonomy of earthly things, the relevance of the Gospel to man's education, to his social economic life, to his political life, to the problems of living that beset him; the urgency of these problems can hardly fail to bring us together to confront them in common.

The Council's Pastoral Constitution exhorts all the Catholic faithful to recognize the signs of the times – an expression which recurs in the Decree *On Ecumenism.* But while this decree fully recognizes the value and opportuneness of a common concern and a 'more intensive cooperation carrying out any duties for the common good of humanity which are demanded by Christian conscience', it does not put this first. Let me quote again:

In ecumenical work Catholics must assuredly be concerned for their separated brethren, praying for them, keeping them informed about the Church, making the first approaches to them; but their primary duty is to make a careful and honest appraisal of whatever needs to be renewed and done in the Catholic household itself in order that its life may bear witness more clearly and faithfully to the teachings and institutions which have been handed down from Christ through the apostles.

In going on to speak of the practice of ecumenism which 'involves the whole Church, faithful and clergy alike,' the Decree quickly reverts to this point:

every renewal of the Church essentially consists in an increase of fidelity to her own calling. Undoubtedly this explains the dynamism of the movement towards Unity.

The humility generated by this spiritual ecumenism will provide a proper frame of mind for dialogue and for the study which is the absolute pre-requisite of dialogue. The Decree reminds us too that not only is dialogue not exhausted in such conversations as our own but also that these conversations cannot be sustained indefinitely except against a background of wide ecumenical education.

I need not remind you of the famous sentence in Chapter 3 which assigns a special place to the Anglican Communion –

surely because it manifests to such a degree those criteria
already adumbrated in *De Ecclesia* 15 and more fully developed here. The culminating reason why we are present here
today is that this 'special place' was thrown into such sharp
relief by the meeting last March of Pope Paul VI and the
Archbishop of Canterbury. It was not the first time that the
present Pontiff had shown his special regard for the Anglican
Communion, but it was unique in its impact. You will remember that he praised the spontaneity and wise courage of the
Archbishop as well as his *pietas*. Let us remember all the
ancient overtones of that word *pietas*. The Archbishop's confidence was indeed well judged for, as the Pope said, his steps
did not echo in a strange house.

Our own meeting is a product of that more famous meeting.
Let us not forget the extent to which the programme we are
setting out to draw up has already been determined in its
essential character at this earlier meeting. Our task is to formulate grave and complex problems in such a way that we
may study and meditate upon them together, without resentment born of pride, without thought of earthly advantage,
in obedience to the words of Christ and with the help of the
Holy Spirit.

4

Where Should Dialogue Begin?

A PAPER READ AT GAZZADA, 10 JANUARY 1967

PROFESSOR EUGENE R. FAIRWEATHER

Prefatory note

This paper attempts to survey, as comprehensively as the subject requires, yet as succinctly as the occasion demands, the areas which must be covered in any serious theological dialogue between the Roman Catholic Church and the Anglican Church. The limited time available both for preparation and for presentation has meant that I have necessarily dealt very summarily with a wide range of important issues: indeed, I have had to refrain from exploring any single question in depth, since to do so would be to throw the whole paper out of balance. Nevertheless, I hope that I have at least managed to say enough about each question to indicate its importance for any adequate dialogue between our two communions.

I. *Introductory*

Before making any attempt to indicate the crucial substantive issues of our dialogue, I must try to define the standpoint from which this survey will be made. First, then, I shall note what I take to be an indispensable condition of fruitful ecumenical dialogue. Secondly, I shall try to state the position from which the Anglican Communion approaches dialogue with Roman Catholics. Finally, I shall list, as summarily as possible, the matters which, over the past four centuries, have become points of serious conflict between us. When all this has been done, it should be possible to make an informed analysis of the really crucial issues.

1. *The approach to dialogue: dialogue and renewal*

True ecumenical dialogue demands commitment to the renewal of our own ecclesiastical life. As long as we take it for granted that all is for the best in the best of all possible churches – namely, our own – there is no real hope of corporate reconciliation. It is only when a particular church is ready to cast a critical eye on its own past and present realization of the Gospel, as well as on the doctrine and life of other churches, that it can pass from monologue to dialogue.

Happily, both the Roman Catholic Church and the Anglican Church have at least begun to practise the self-criticism required for genuine dialogue. That we have done so is indeed no occasion for self-congratulation. At least two circumstances have forced us to reassess our actual teaching and practice. On the one hand, as we have entered, however cautiously, into the modern ecumenical movement, we have discovered that what seems obviously true and right to us is far from self-evident to sincere Christians of other traditions; as a result, we have had to ask ourselves whether our conventional theologies, usages and structures do justice to our own received standards, or even whether our traditional formularies themselves are the clearest and most balanced statements of the profound truths of our faith that we are capable of providing. On the other hand, we have been forced by the undeniable crisis of the Christian mission in the modern world to ask what is essential and enduring and what is expendable and transient in the complex of ideas, customs and institutions which constitute our tradition. Thanks to the pressure of these circumstances we have been more willing than in the past to accept the guidance of the Holy Spirit of unity, and as a result we have ceased to address one another from totally immovable positions.

This unmistakable change of attitude on the part of both churches does not, of course, guarantee a successful outcome to our quest for unity. In so far as commitment to self-criticism and renewal does involve a thoroughgoing effort to distinguish between the central and the peripheral, between the reality of the Gospel and the Church and the conceptual vocabulary and organizational forms in which that reality is expressed and embodied at any given moment, we may not unreasonably expect that our common involvement in the task of renewal will take us a long way towards a point of convergence. We cannot, however, ask that self-criticism should extend to the repudiation of either communion's clearest vision of the reality of Gospel and Church, since that would be to ask some or all of us to compromise the faith by which we live. Consequently, we must face the possibility that we may come to a point where we can only wait and pray for fuller light. At the same time, we must not exclude the possibility that a sufficiently radical examination and a sufficiently lucid exposition of the faith by which the Roman Catholic Church lives and the faith by which the Anglican Church lives will eventually make it plain to us both that we live by the same Christian and Catholic faith.

(I hope it is clear that I am not advocating the formulation of a minimal agreement on the ground common to our existing standards of doctrine and discipline – or, *a fortiori*, on the ground common to our current theological interpretations and practical applications of those standards. Such an agreement would, in the nature of the case, fail to do justice to the legitimate concerns of either communion. What I am suggesting is that we should ask what crucial Christian truth our formularies are designed to express – as distinct from the partial, and often polemical, form in which that truth is actually expressed.)

2. *The Anglican position in dialogue with Roman Catholics*

I turn now from this brief comment on the state of mind required for fruitful ecumenical dialogue to an equally brief account of the contents of the Anglican mind as it approaches dialogue with Roman Catholics. It goes without saying that I do not claim that the Anglican mind at this moment possesses the full and undistorted truth concerning either the Gospel or Roman Catholicism. It is essential, however, that we should all see, as clearly as possible, just where the Anglican Communion now stands and in what perspective Anglicans now view the Roman Catholic Church. It is our real selves, rather than some idealized image, that we must bring to the dialogue.

As any informed observer will realize, it is not at all easy
to describe the Anglican attitude towards Roman Catholicism.
The received Anglican formularies, interpreted rigorously
and with due recognition of their moments of ambiguity, leave
open a fairly wide range of attitudes on this and many other
matters, and it must be acknowledged that Anglicans have
not been slow to exercise their freedom. Thus different Anglicans or groups of Anglicans have held and hold significantly
different views of the Roman Catholic Church. Nevertheless,
it is not impossible to present a coherent outline of these views,
since they do stem from a common root.

Very simply described, that common root is the appeal to
the apostolic witness, embodied in Scripture, and to the con-
tinuous witness of the Church, given above all in the ancient
Creeds and in the judgments of the Ecumenical Councils received by East and West alike, as the basis of doctrinal statement, and the parallel appeal to apostolic order, reflected in
Scripture and in the Fathers of the Church, as the primary
guide to liturgical practice and to polity. This dual appeal is
clearly implied in the earliest formularies of 'separate' Anglicanism, it is fully developed by the greatest Anglican apolo-
gists, and the readiness to function within the limits which it
imposes is the basis of Anglican unity.

On its negative side, the Anglican criterion of faith and
order, just summarized, involves the rejection of other alleged-
ly definitive authorities, including both medieval and later
Western Councils and the Roman See itself. It is common
Anglican teaching that neither the definitions of the medieval
Councils, Trent, and the First Vatican Council, nor the acts
of the Roman Pontiffs (however instructive either may sometimes prove) are binding on the Christian conscience. They
are not binding, it is held, because in both cases they are *ultra
vires*. Consequently, neither Western conciliar nor papal
dogmatic definitions can be regarded by Anglicans as *de fide*.

Especially in view of the fact that the post-Reformation
Anglican Church has not believed itself entitled to define and
impose dogmas of its own, this rejection of the medieval and
Tridentine accumulation of dogmatic statements has necessarily resulted in a doctrinal openness (or 'comprehensiveness')
which has come to be recognized as a characteristic note of

Anglicanism. As far as Anglican/Roman Catholic relations
are concerned, this openness has permitted the development
of a variety of Anglican attitudes (all of which, however, naturally retain as their common basis the rejection of medieval
Western and modern Roman Catholic dogma precisely as
dogma). These attitudes must now be summarily presented.

(i) One school of Anglican theologians, securely rooted in
Anglican history, tends to look favourably on many (or even
most) medieval and modern Roman doctrinal statements as,
at any rate in their historical context, acceptable expressions of
a sound theology. Theologians of this type may well find themselves very close to their Roman Catholic colleagues in their
handling of such prickly themes as grace and the sacraments
– and that without any disloyalty to the Anglican dogmatic
position. It must be observed, however, that such theologians
are representative of the Anglican Communion and its tradition only in so far as they continue to question the dogmatic
force of the doctrinal definitions with which we are concerned
here.

(ii) Other theologians, no less genuinely Anglican, are less
positive in their estimate of the same definitions. They may
indeed share the convictions underlying many of these formulations, but they will criticize the actual statements as often
too narrowly Western in their treatment of a given subject,
as at least occasionally appearing to give too great authority
to 'scholastic' philosophical categories, or (in certain instances)
as canonizing speculations to which Scripture, Creeds, Councils and Fathers give no visible support. Such theologians,
then, not only question the dogmatic authority of medieval
and modern Roman definitions, but also find their method and
idiom more or less uncongenial.

(iii) Other theologians again, speaking out of an established
tradition of Anglican theology and churchmanship, will be
essentially negative in their judgment of some, if not all, of
these definitions. Wholeheartedly accepting, as they do, the
concerns and convictions of the Reformation regarding the
substance of the Gospel, they believe that the Protestant
critique of medieval dogma and theology was basically sound,
and they do not find the decrees of Trent reassuring. Theologians of this type, then, not only query the dogmatic status

of medieval and modern Roman definitions and criticize their style and categories, but also tend to see in the convictions expressed in them a misinterpretation of the Gospel.

To the outside observer it may seem very strange indeed that a Western church, deeply involved in the theological conflicts and the political plots and counterplots of the sixteenth century, should have emerged into the modern world without having definitively resolved for its own members some of the thorniest questions of the Reformation and Counter-Reformation, but for our present purpose it will do us no harm to remain puzzled on this score. It is enough for us to see clearly both the unity and the diversity in the Anglican approach to distinctively Roman Catholic dogmatic formulae. It is to this need alone that I have addressed myself in the few short paragraphs above.

3. *The historic issues of Anglican/Roman Catholic controversy*

As far as Roman Catholic dogma is concerned – and this is surely the crucial area of controversy – it should now be apparent that Anglican criticism has two aspects, a 'formal' and a 'material'. On the one hand, each and every medieval Western or modern Roman Catholic dogmatic definition is queried on the ground of the insufficient authority of the definer. On the other hand, individual dogmatic definitions are more or less widely criticized on account of their content and/or style. It is clear, then, that a useful dialogue will have to cover both the underlying problem of authority and a considerable variety of particular doctrinal questions.

At this point it may be useful to offer at least a hasty survey of the specific questions which have loomed large in the minds of Anglican controversialists. While to ecumenically attuned ears it will no doubt be painful, it should also be instructive to note the grievances recorded by a representative Anglican divine of the so-called 'classical' period. 'Their new creed of Pius IV', wrote the Cambridge divine, Isaac Barrow, 'containeth these novelties and heterodoxies. 1 *Seven sacraments.* 2. *Trent doctrine of justification and original sin.* 3. *Propitiatory sacrifice of the mass.* 4. *Transubstantiation.* 5. *Communicating under one kind.* 6. *Purgatory.* 7. *Invocation of saints.*

8. *Veneration of relics.* 9. *Worship of images.* 10. *The Roman church to be the mother and mistress of all churches.* 11. *Swearing obedience to the pope.* 12. *Receiving the decrees of all synods,* and of Trent.[1] To this list we may add the titles of two tracts selected from Vol. III of Cardwell's compendium: William Sherlock, *A Discourse concerning a Judge of Controversies in Matters of Religion;* Simon Patrick, *A Discourse about Tradition: shewing what is meant by it, and what Tradition is to be Received, and what Tradition is to be Rejected.*

Turning to more recent developments, we may note, finally, the Anglican opposition to the definitions of the Immaculate Conception and Assumption of the Blessed Virgin, the rejection of the dogma of papal infallibility, and the criticism of such actions as the condemnation of Anglican orders and the enforcement of the strict rules concerning mixed marriages.

It will be seen that both 'formal' and 'material' questions are well represented in this list. It seems obvious that the 'formal' aspect of the total problem is the more fundamental one. Let us devise two examples. It is theoretically conceivable that every living Anglican might be persuaded by theological argument that the doctrine of the Assumption was probably true, but this would count for little in Roman Catholic eyes as long as Anglicans continued to maintain that the doctrine had no discoverable basis in Scripture and that in any case Pope Pius XII had no right to define it. It is also conceivable that Roman Catholics might review the question of Anglican orders with positive results, but this would not be an effective step towards corporate reunion unless the basic issue of papal authority was somehow resolved. At the same time, it is impossible to isolate the 'formal' from the 'material' issues. The claims of a particular person or institution to authority can hardly be discussed rationally altogether apart from some agreement as to the general compatibility of his or its utterances with already recognized authorities or with a reasonable view of the world. Moreover, each step towards agreement, however minor, contributes to mutual confidence, and therefore to better dialogue. Thus the most promising plan for

---

1. *A Treatise of the Pope's Supremacy*, ed. E. Cardwell, *Enchiridion Theologicum Anti-Romanum*, Vol. II (Oxford: University Press, 1852), p. 427.

dialogue would seem to be one which provided for the more or less concurrent discussion of 'formal' and 'material' issues.

Nevertheless, the 'formal' questions possess a certain logical priority, and they must surely for that reason be pursued intensively from the beginning of our dialogue. Furthermore, it is highly probable that, as the centuries have passed, the 'formal' issues have come to play a larger and the 'material' issues a smaller part in shaping the attitude of most Anglicans towards the Roman Catholic Church. (For one thing, Anglican concern with the 'formal' issues was significantly increased by the definition of papal infallibility in 1870. Interestingly enough, that definition was promulgated at a time when many Anglicans were coming to take a more positive view of the Tridentine decrees, and it must be said that its promulgation was something of a setback to that development.) Consequently, it will be especially important for our Anglican/Roman Catholic dialogue to keep the 'formal' questions constantly in our minds.

(It will have been observed that the standard list of points of controversy includes a number of matters of discipline as well as of dogma – e.g. communion in one kind, marriage discipline. While such matters may be technically separable from dogmatic questions, they do in fact bear on what we might call 'dogmatic realities' – e.g. the sacraments of the Eucharist and of matrimony – and in my view they will be most effectively handled in the context of a properly theological, rather than a purely canonical, study.)

II. *The key issues*

I turn now to a rapid survey of what I take to be the key questions at issue between Anglicans and Roman Catholics both in the past and to a great extent, albeit with important changes of emphasis, in the present. In my present judgment, at any rate, the issues which have dominated the Anglican/Roman Catholic debate throughout its history are two in number, one 'formal' and one 'material'. Admittedly, the classical Anglican works of controversy cover a much longer list of topics, but I believe that the primary issues can be reduced to two, and that other questions are matters of controversy principally because these two issues, in one way or another, enter into them. For ready reference I have identified the 'formal' issue as 'the authority of Christian doctrine' and the 'material' issue as 'the nature of the Gospel'. I plan to sketch each problem in turn, before I go on to make positive proposals for the ordering of our dialogue.

1. *The authority of Christian doctrine*

Any church, passing through such a crisis as the Church of England experienced in the sixteenth century, is driven to raise the question of the authenticity of its message. Christianity being a religion of revelation, that question must inevitably be put in this precise form: By what authority do we teach a given doctrine as true? What is the relation of any doctrinal formula to the revelation of God in Christ? If the influence of the Reformation is strong (as it was in the Church of England in the early decades of its separate history), the same question is likely to be expressed in some such form as this: How do we know that we are preaching the pure Word of God? How do human words communicate the divine Word? These problems were significant for the separation between Rome and Canterbury; presumably they will also prove significant for the projected dialogue between Rome and Canterbury.

(a) *Scripture and Tradition*

The Anglican Church has never denied all authority to Tradition. On the contrary, it has appealed to Tradition in support of its ordering of its liturgy and its hierarchy, and it has referred to Councils and Fathers as authorities for its teaching. At the same time, it has clearly and repeatedly asserted what we may call the 'material sufficiency' of Scripture for the establishment of Christian doctrine.

The Anglican concern here is clear enough. Authentic Christianity depends essentially on God's self-disclosure. Anglicans are convinced that the only dependable evidence for the events of divine revelation is to be found in Scripture (or possibly in the primitive Christian confessions of faith, which in fact add nothing to the substance of Scripture). Consequently, while they recognize the value of Tradition for the interpretation of the biblical message, they consistently reject Tradition as an independent source of information about the facts of the Gospel. Even in the case of Christian institutions they do not appeal to Tradition to validate an order which has no *point d'appui* in Scripture. Consequently, Anglicans have consistently questioned what they have (not without reason) taken to be the prevailing view among Roman Catholics – namely, that extra-scriptural Tradition can properly be treated as a distinct channel of divine truth, independent of Scripture.

(b) The structure of ecclesiastical authority

The Anglican Communion has never repudiated the teaching authority of the Church. On the contrary, it has affirmed that authority in general terms; it has specifically accepted the decrees of the first four Ecumenical Councils as a test of orthodox doctrine; it has acknowledged the role of the Church as interpreter of Scripture. At the same time, it has insisted on Scripture itself as the primary norm of the Church's teaching, while refusing to ascribe what we might call an 'official infallibility' to any person or institution within the Church.

The concern which we have already noted reappears here. True Christian faith rests on divine, not on merely human, teaching. According to the Anglican view, the teaching authority of the Church is indeed a safeguard against purely individual and arbitrary interpretations of Scripture – i.e. against merely human teaching. But the Church's teaching itself must be safeguarded against human corruptions, and Anglicans find the required protection in the recognition of the primacy of Scripture and in the denial of institutional or personal infallibility. When Anglican theologians undertake to develop a theory of ecclesiastical authority in matters of faith, they tend to correlate very closely the collective voice of the episcopate and the *consensus fidelium*, so as to avoid any suggestion of the inherent infallibility of councils.

(c) The exercise of authority in doctrine

While the Anglican Communion has not lacked speculative theologians, it has refrained from producing elaborate doctrinal statements, couched in the language of speculative theology, and its theologians have consistently been critical of any suggestion that theology can explain the mysteries of the faith with the help of the categories of speculative philosophy. Furthermore, while the Apostles' and Nicene Creeds are regularly recited in public worship and the decrees of the First Council of Nicaea and subsequent councils are recognized as standards of orthodox belief, Anglican authorities have shown themselves hesitant to restrict theological reflection and exposition by any rigid insistence on the thought-forms of the patristic age. Indeed, the Anglican Communion as a whole is notoriously slow to impose any formal discipline on theologians who are seriously trying to interpret and present the received Christian faith in a fresh idiom, however novel that idiom may appear to be.

This cautious and gentle approach to the exercise of doctrinal authority is a further expression of the concern for truth, to which I have referred above. The Anglican tradition embodies a strong sense of the transcendent mystery of the true God and of the danger of pretending to describe the ineffable in his being or his action. At times this awareness may seem to have resulted in an almost complete disuse of ecclesiastical authority in doctrine – though of course it should be remembered that the *lex orandi* of the Book of Common Prayer has remained at all times as an effectual *lex credendi*. But Anglicans by and large seem less afraid of the partial disuse than of the misuse of doctrinal authority, and they are certainly averse to any large claims to dogmatic certitude. It is clear that they will want to know whether the Roman Catholic attitude towards dogmatic formulations can become more flexible than it is widely supposed to have been in the past.

2. *The nature of the Gospel*

The question of the 'pure Word of God' carries with it, as its natural complement, the question of the message which God speaks in his Word to man. Christianity being a religion of salvation, the question of God's message must primarily be the question of the 'nature of the Gospel'. That question may conveniently be subdivided as follows: Why, and how badly, does man need to hear the Gospel of salvation? By whom, and how, is man saved? To what extent can man participate in the work of his salvation? In the sixteenth century the Anglican Reformers, in common with their Lutheran and Reformed colleagues, felt it necessary to protest strongly against what they at least took to be a widespread Pelagian infection in medieval Latin theology – an infection against which they did not believe that papal authority was prepared to take strong enough measures.

The suspicion that Roman Catholic theology does not take the depth of man's sinfulness and the completeness of his dependence on God's grace with sufficient seriousness has lingered in the Anglican mind – despite (or perhaps because of) its own tendency, in certain moods, to lapse into a thoroughgoing Pelagianism! – and it has influenced Anglican views of more than one aspect of the Roman Catholic tradition. For example, the strong and widespread hostility within Anglicanism to certain features of Marian doctrine and piety and to the idea of the Mass as a 'propitiatory sacrifice' does not stem from a total denial of Mary's place in the history of salvation or of the sacrificial aspect of the Eucharist, let alone from irreverence towards the Blessed Virgin or the Blessed Sacrament. It is motivated rather by the fear that man's part in the work of his salvation will be exaggerated and God's part minimized. This fear (whether justified or not) will have to be taken into account in any realistic dialogue between Anglicans and Roman Catholics.

(a) The condition of man

The Anglican Communion has never taught a doctrine of the 'total depravity' of fallen man. It has never been willing to use the kind of language about human reason and human works which apparently came easily to the lips of Lutherans and Calvinists (though admittedly individual Anglican theologians can be found who used such language readily). Nevertheless, Anglicans have commonly been critical of the treatment by Roman Catholic theology of the doctrine of the fall and original sin. In particular, they have criticized any use of the concept of a *donum superadditum naturae* which seemed to minimize the effects of the fall on the workings of human nature. Moreover, they have tended to interpret official

Roman Catholic statements in the light of the mildest scholastic accounts of the fall and original sin. They may indeed have been led by polemical fervour into exaggeration and misrepresentation, but it is at all events clear that the issue will need to be explored.

(b) *The Redemption of man*

The Anglican Communion has never questioned the part played by human nature, in the person of the incarnate Word, in the work of man's Redemption. Anglican theology has revealed no sympathy with Monothelitism or with any other doctrine which would minimize the reality and the salvific role of Christ's human will and his other human powers. At the same time, it has been concerned to safeguard the fundamental truth that God alone is man's Redeemer and that no mere man is able to save himself, let alone anyone else. It is this concern that has made Anglicans critical of any Mariological thesis or of any aspect of the cult of Mary and the saints which might seem to compromise the Gospel of Redemption. For example, the description of Mary as *mediatrix,* even when it is duly qualified (as in *Lumen Gentium,* no. 60), creates serious difficulties for Anglicans. Similar difficulties would be raised by any interpretation of the eucharistic sacrifice which appeared to detract from the full efficacy of the sacrifice of Jesus Christ. The problems noted here will obviously have to be borne in mind in any future discussion of Mariology or of sacramental theology.

(c) *Redeemed man*

The Anglican Communion has never denied the reality of man's sanctification by the grace of Christ, nor has it questioned the role of good works in man's attainment of his final destiny. On the contrary, it has filled its liturgical texts with calls to holiness, with confessions of God's sanctifying power, with prayers for grace to perform the good works which are integral to the Christian life. At the same time, Anglican theology has commonly insisted on the aspect of 'imputation' in the justification of man – not in order to construct a doctrine which would in effect make sanctification and good

works extrinsic to the effectual work of salvation, but with a
view to safeguarding the truth that man can never really earn
his salvation, which for ever remains dependent on the forgiv-
ing love of God. Unfortunately, at least some Roman Catholic
presentations of the meaning of grace (e.g. certain interpretations of grace in terms of the category of *habitus*), of justification and of merit have appeared to Anglicans to corrupt or
obscure this truth. It is obvious that this aspect of the doctrine
of grace will need to be clarified at some point in our dialogue.

III. *Starting-point for dialogue: Revelation and the Church*

Part II of this paper was of necessity largely negative in
tone. I hope it is unnecessary to explain that in writing it I
was not trying to convince Roman Catholics of the error of
their ways. My purpose was purely and simply to lay on the
table the principal difficulties which Roman Catholic teaching
and practice, as Anglicans have understood them, have presented to some, many, or all Anglicans through the centuries
since the Reformation. If any of these difficulties should prove
to have arisen from careless language on the Roman Catholic
side or misunderstanding on the Anglican side, we may happily pass over them and work on the problems that remain. I
have put them forward only because they do exist at present, at
least in Anglican minds, and there is no point in proceeding to
dialogue until the existing weighty difficulties have been
brought to light. I turn now to some specific proposals for the
pattern of our dialogue, based on my analysis of the major
problems. While these proposals are not exhaustive, I believe
that they do cover the most sensitive areas in Anglican/Roman
Catholic relations. Partly because of limited space and partly
because the issues to which these proposals are addressed have
already been outlined, my suggested plan will be very summarily sketched. If it seems useful, it will be possible to expand
this sketch later on.

As I observed in Part I of this paper, a happy sign of our
times is the fact that neither the Roman Catholic Church nor
the Anglican Church can any longer be accused of standing
frozen in a position of unshakable self-satisfaction. Both chur-

ches have at least begun to respond to the call to that renewal which is so urgently needed if they are to meet the needs of the Christian life and the Christian mission in our time. In both churches new modes of thought and new patterns of action are winning their way.

It seems nothing less than providential that this renewal should already have touched both Roman Catholic and Anglican views of the problem which I have described as the key 'formal' issue for Anglican/Roman Catholic dialogue. On the one hand, in its two great dogmatic constitutions, *Dei Verbum* and *Lumen Gentium*, Vatican II has both set the old question of Scripture and Tradition in a new perspective and presented the reality of the Church in a way which sheds new light on the question of ecclesiastical authority. On the other hand, Anglicans, drawing both on the neglected resources of their own tradition, and on the results of recent biblical and historical research and ecumenical dialogue, seem to be moving, less spectacularly but not less surely, towards a point of convergence with these important trends in contemporary Roman Catholic thought. My first proposal, therefore, is that we should build our dialogue on what has already been accomplished and proceed to a common study of the themes which I have labelled 'Revelation and Tradition' and 'The Nature and Structure of the Church'.

1. *Revelation and Tradition*

In the constitution *Dei Verbum* the Second Vatican Council has provided both Roman Catholicism and the entire Christian world with a fresh and substantial treatise on the basis of Christian doctrine and theology, ranging from the concept of revelation itself, through the significance of Tradition, Scripture and the Church's teaching office, to the exercise of doctrinal authority. As it happens, the constitution's main ideas on most of these points come very close to the conclusions which representative Anglican, Protestant and Orthodox theologians have reached or are approaching. Common reflection on the broad theme of *Dei Verbum* should therefore be a promising point of departure for dialogue on the outstanding points of difference.

(a) *The nature of Revelation*

A more integrally personal and less verbalistic, abstract and formal notion of revelation has come to the fore in present-day theology, both Roman Catholic and non-Roman Catholic. This development opens the way to the reconsideration of such questions as the transmission of revelation and the nature and exercise of ecclesiastical authority, particularly in the doctrinal sphere.

(b) *Tradition and Scripture*

Modern biblical, historical and theological studies have rendered obsolete the rigid dualism of Scripture and Tradition which bedevilled theological teaching and controversy in the age of the Reformation and Counter-Reformation. Moreover, in a time when a Roman Catholic dogmatic constitution on divine revelation and its transmission can devote more than half its space to the Bible and its interpretation, while a Faith and Order Conference of the World Council of Churches (Montreal, 1963) can consider with equanimity the formula *sola traditione*, it is clear that old controversial stereotypes have lost whatever relevance they once had. Surely this new situation is a compelling invitation to dialogue.

(c) *Tradition and the magisterium*

If consensus can be reached on a personal, rather than a narrowly conceptual, view of revelation, and on a communal rather than an atomistic view of the transmission of revelation, a profitable review of the nature and institutional form of the Church's teaching office should be feasible. In particular, it should be easier than it has been in the past to avoid an excessively juridical interpretation and performance of the Church's teaching function.

(d) *The nature of doctrinal statements*

On the same basis, the nature of dogmatic formulations can readily be conceived in a less 'fundamentalist' way – i.e. with less preoccupation with the verbal forms of dogma – than has been the case in most churches in recent centuries. Such a change of emphasis could be of major importance for the reconsideration of past and present dogmatic conflicts.

2. *The nature and structure of the Church*

In the constitution *Lumen Gentium* the Second Vatican Council has promulgated a solid treatise on ecclesiology, ranging from a basic description of the Church as Body of Christ and People of God, through a full discussion of its institutional structure and an extended treatment of its vocation to holiness, to a presentation of its eschatological destiny. The constitution on the Church, as its teaching is assimilated by Roman Catholic theology, will inevitably bring the latter into close rapport with living Anglican, Protestant and Orthodox thought. Common study of the broad theme of *Lumen Gentium* should therefore be an advantageous starting-point for dialogue on the outstanding points of difference in the area of ecclesiology.

(a) *The mystery of the Church*

A more organic and mystical and less institutional and external view of the Church has been rapidly gaining ground in present-day ecclesiology, both Roman Catholic and non-Roman Catholic. This shift of perspective should make possible a fresh and fruitful investigation of such controversial questions as the nature of the ecclesiastical hierarchy and the relation of papal authority (which Roman Catholics alone affirm) to episcopal authority (which is common ground for the Roman Church and other episcopal churches).

(b) *The apostolic foundation of the Church*

From the Anglican standpoint, at any rate, an approach to the question of the ecclesiastical hierarchy through a study of the apostolic mission, in which the Church itself was constituted, promises to be worthwhile – affirming as it does the distinctive authority of the ordained ministry in the Church without making that ministry external to the Church. *Lumen Gentium* thus supplies a good starting-point for dialogue on the nature and status of the hierarchy.

(c) *Apostolic episcopate and Petrine primacy*

Discussion of the hierarchy, and especially of the episcopal college, in relation to the mission of the apostles, leads naturally into consideration of the primatial claims of the Roman bishops as successors of St. Peter. It seems safe to predict that the question of papal primacy and infallibility will be the thorniest issue in our entire dialogue. If a solution can be reached, however, I make bold to suggest that its basis will be found in a deeper exploration of the New Testament evidence for the establishment of the apostolate and in fuller reflection on the nature of the episcopal college, as based on the apostolate.

IV. *Dialogue continued: grace and the sacraments*

When we turn to what I have called the key 'material' issue for Anglican/Roman Catholic dialogue, we shall find that much less significant progress has been made towards a preliminary consensus, and in particular that we have no major document of Vatican II to help us forward. (The two partial exceptions to this generalization are the Marian question and the problem of the eucharistic sacrifice.) None the less, hopeful stirrings can be detected in this area of theology, and it seems likely that new resources will present themselves as we proceed with our dialogue. In any case, as I have already pointed out (in Part II above), the issue is too important to be ignored. I suggest, therefore, that at some point we undertake a common study of 'Grace and the Sacraments', with attention at least to those aspects of the problem which I have labelled 'The Doctrine of Grace', 'The Doctrine of Penance', 'Marian Doctrine and Devotion', and 'Sacramental Questions'.

1. *The doctrine of grace*

A common mind on the fundamental question of the relation between nature and grace is clearly the prerequisite of real mutual understanding on certain of the most controversial issues of the past. As I have already suggested in Part II of this paper, this problem underlies many of the historic disputes between Anglicans and Roman Catholics.

(a) *The meaning of grace*

To begin with, it will be important to clarify the significance of grace as God's act and gift, which never becomes man's pos-

session apart from his personal relation to God. Here we shall
find – most fortunately for our purpose – that the interest of
modern Roman Catholic theology in the doctrine of *gratia
increata* coincides with long-standing concerns of Anglican
theologians.

(b) The effects of grace

Clarification of our understanding of the gracious action of
God towards man will be a further essential step. Happily,
there is reason to suppose that, in the light of modern biblical
studies in particular, a way can be found to transcend the old
controversies concerning justification and sanctification.

(c) Grace and merit

The effect of man's good works under the influence of grace
has long been expressed in Latin theology in terms of a notion
of merit which, at least to Anglican ears, too easily suggests
that man can really earn his standing before God, and is therefore not constantly dependent on divine grace. It would be
useful to explore this question in common, with a view to ascer-
taining whether a less juridical and extrinsic mode of expression would not alleviate this difficulty.

2. The doctrine of penance

Under the same general rubric of the relation between
divine and human action certain specific questions arise,
which may be grouped under the heading of 'The Doctrine
of Penance'. These questions all relate to certain uses of the
notion of satisfaction in Latin theology, and they all have
created difficulties in the past. It will be important for us to
explore these questions together.

(a) 'Temporal punishment'

In the first place, it will be necessary to ask whether the
terminology of 'penalty' or 'punishment' is the most suitable
idiom in which to express the theological meaning of peniten-
tial discipline, or whether a less juridical and more personal
vocabulary might not be less misleading. The root of the problem seems to lie here.

(b) *Penance and absolution*

A related question is that of the connection between the imposition of a 'penance' and the giving of absolution. Since the Roman Catholic requirement of a penance has no parallel in Orthodox or Anglican standards, it would be ecumenically useful to discover just what theological considerations are involved in the Roman practice.

(c) *Purgatory*

The application of the idea of 'temporal penalty' to Roman Catholic eschatology, in the form of the developed doctrine of purgatory, is a matter not merely of difference but of active controversy between Roman Catholics and other Christians (including both Anglicans and Orthodox). It will sooner or later be necessary to explore this question, preferably in the present context of the theology of penance.

(d) *Indulgences*

While the practice of indulgences is no longer a focal point of bitter controversy (as it was, of course, at the time of the Reformation), the theory of indulgences, like the doctrine of purgatory, remains a stumbling-block to Anglicans, Orthodox and others. It will be necessary, then, to include this question in our discussion of the notion of satisfaction and its implications.

3. *Marian doctrine and devotion*

It is appropriate to consider the Marian question under the heading of 'The Doctrine of Grace', since it is ultimately the fear (justified or otherwise) that Mary will be regarded as a source rather than a recipient and instrument of grace that has led, at least in the non-Roman Catholic West, to prolonged distrust and controversy. More precisely, it is the tendency to assimilate Mary to Christ in a way which seems to isolate her from the Church's other members – e.g. in the development of a doctrine of 'co-redemption' – that arouses deep fears. In the case of certain Marian doctrines, the problem of ecclesiastical authority is also involved. The whole issue will obviously have to be discussed fully in the course of our dialogue.

(a) *Mary and the Redemption of man*

As it happens, in *Lumen Gentium*, chapter VIII, Vatican II has supplied us with a helpful starting-point for dialogue on Marian doctrine and devotion. In its main outlines, at any rate, the interpretation of Mary's role in the history of salvation worked out in *Lumen Gentium* coincides with views widely held in classical Anglican theology. We may thus hope to find at least some common ground at the very beginning of our discussion of this question.

(b) *Mary in Christian devotion*

The same constitution also gives us a useful starting-point for the discussion of Marian devotion. Both Roman Catholics and Anglicans should find it instructive to explore together, with the help of *Lumen Gentium*, the question of the appropriate expressions of our common reverence for the Blessed Virgin Mary.

(c) *The modern Marian definitions*

By reason both of their content and of their manner of promulgation, the definitions of 1854 and 1950 have undoubtedly complicated the relations of other Christians with the Roman Catholic Church. Our dialogue should explore thoroughly both the relation of these dogmas to other widely accepted dogmas and the grounds on which the Roman See has defined them as dogmas.

4. *Sacramental questions*

In view of the extensive ferment in contemporary thinking about the sacraments, our dialogue might well contribute to the enlightenment both of Roman Catholic and of Anglican theologians if it included a comprehensive discussion of sacramental theology and practice. The most urgent questions, however, seem to be those which are more or less directly related to the issue of nature and grace – although we shall have to add one further question which constitutes an immediate practical problem for Anglican/Roman Catholic relations.

(a) The nature and number of the sacraments

Past and present controversies on the subject make it essential for us to explore fully the meaning of sacramental actions as effectual signs of divine grace. On the one hand, it will be important for us to distinguish this doctrine clearly from any notion of a sacrament as an instrument for human manipulation of grace. (Past debates on the formula *ex opere operato* may well prove instructive here.) On the other hand, we must try to uncover the concern underlying past insistence on the unique sacramental status of Baptism and the Eucharist – even though modern biblical and historical studies have already put the question in a somewhat different light. To my mind, that essential concern was quite clearly the concern that the doctrine and practice, both of the 'sacraments of the Gospel' and of the five rites 'commonly called sacraments', should be conformed strictly to the revealed purpose of the God of grace.

(b) Eucharistic sacrifice and presence

During the past four centuries, two crucial doctrinal questions concerning the Eucharist have been repeatedly raised. In the one case – that of the eucharistic sacrifice – the heart of the controversy was clearly the fear (on the part of Anglicans and Protestants) that human action would somehow be construed as supplementing the self-oblation of Christ. In the other case – that of the eucharistic presence – while other considerations have come into play, the most persistent criticism of the dogma of transubstantiation as an interpretation of the eucharistic presence has stemmed from a deep suspicion of the formula as a rationalistic intrusion into the sacramental mystery. In the light of modern studies in eucharistic theology, it should be possible for us to carry on a fruitful dialogue on both these issues.

(c) The Christian priesthood

The problem of the eucharistic sacrifice has played a major role in Anglican/Roman Catholic controversy concerning the priesthood (including the prolonged debate on Anglican orders). The extensive studies already carried out in both churches on the eucharistic sacrifice and the nature and function of priesthood should provide a firm basis for dialogue. In my judgment, it will not be profitable to discuss the validity of Anglican ordinations until the doctrines of the Eucharist and the Christian priesthood have been fully considered.

(d) *The doctrine and discipline of Christian marriage*

The rapidly changing conditions of modern society have at least contributed to the raising, in most Christian communions, of a number of questions concerning the theology and the ethics of Christian marriage. Dialogue on the question of marriage, in all its aspects, should therefore be of real benefit to both Anglicans and Roman Catholics. It is probable that the practical problems connected with 'mixed marriages' can most profitably be discussed in this wider context.

Concluding note

The above proposals, while summarily presented, are none the less quite specific. Obviously, I cannot (and do not) presume to offer them as anything like a definitive agenda for our dialogue. I believe, none the less, that all these issues will have to be faced in the course of our work together.

5

To What Extent Can or Should There Be Diversity in a United Church?

Freedom and Authority

A PAPER PRESENTED AT HUNTERCOMBE,
1 SEPTEMBER 1967

BISHOP J. G. M. WILLEBRANDS

Some theological considerations

In the Creed of Constantinople (381) we confess 'Credimus in unam sanctam catholicam et apostolicam Ecclesiam' ('We believe in one, holy, catholic and apostolic Church' – Πιστεύομεν εἰς μίαν ἁγίαν καθολικὴν καὶ ἀποστολικὴν Ἐκκλησίαν).

'Credimus', we believe. Though the text of the Latin liturgy has the singular, 'Credo', the original text has the plural 'Credimus'. We are not dealing with an individual. It is a people that believes. The Church, founded by Christ, is continually realized afresh in us by an act of faith. 'It has pleased God . . . to make men holy and save not merely as individuals . . . but by making them into a single people.' [1]

A people means a multitude, and in a certain sense a diversity, by its diversity of function, by its continuity in history. At the same time a people means a racial, spiritual, cultural unity.

When we speak of the people of God, we mean a people not in the sense of a race of men, but a people by election, by sanctification. In the Old Testament this election was given to the people of Israel, and the People of God was at the same time a

1. The Constitution on the Church, *Lumen Gentium*, of the Second Vatican Council, Nr. 9.

particular race, a nation. By the New Testament in his blood, Christ called into being a new people

made up of Jew and Gentile. . . . For those, who believe in Christ, who are reborn not from a perishable but from an imperishable seed through the Word of the living God (cf. 1 Pet. 1.23), not from the flesh but from water and the Holy Spirit (cf. John 3.5–6), are finally established as 'a chosen race, a royal priesthood, a holy nation, a purchased people . . . You who in times past were not a people, but are now the people of God' (1 Pet. 2.9–10). (*Lumen Gentium*, loc cit.)

This people, though divine, remains a *people* made up of men. But unlike a people in the racial or national sense, it is composed of men coming 'from every nation, from all tribes and peoples and tongues'.[2]

This 'people' then has a wider and more radical diversity than had the people of the Old Testament; it comprises a multitude of 'peoples' in the ordinary sense and its unity, though indeed visible, since it is made up of men, is not material. It is a unity which can come only from him who 'from two hath made one people' (Eph. 2.14).

Christ has established his new covenant not to destroy the diversity of nations and races or to conquer them in a material sense, but to destroy the barrier that divided the Old Testament people, Israel, from others – to embrace all the people of the earth in his redemption and lay open salvation to all, to admit all to the fullness which dwells in himself (cf. Col. 1.19). In other words, the unity of the people of God has no sense except in function of the unity and fullness of the work of salvation willed by Christ, who is Alpha and Omega. All then starts from Christ, and the end of all ecclesiastical institution is to gather all in him.

What are this People's principles of unity?

Holy Scripture shows us, as example and ultimate principle, the unity in the Trinity of divine persons. Christ, sent by the Father 'should die for the nation, and not for the nation only, but to gather into one the children of God who are scat-

2. Apoc. (Rev.) 7.9; cf. *Lumen Gentium* Nr. 13: 'It follows that among all the nations on earth there is but one People of God.' 'Not only, then, is the People of God made up of different peoples . . .'

tered abroad' (John 11.51 ff.). His last prayer was 'that they may all be one' (John 17.21). He founded the New Testament in his blood and left to His church the sacramental sign of this covenant in the mystery of the Eucharist by which the unity of the church is signified and brought about (cf. *Lumen Gentium*, Nr. 3).

The Holy Spirit, who proceeds from the Father and the Son, who was sent into the world by the Son, to teach us the fullness of truth, to tell us of the riches of Christ (John 16. 7; 13.15), he creates in us that new life by which we are the people of God, 'regenerati ex aqua et Spiritu Sancto' ('reborn from water and the Holy Spirit'): the 'aqua' is Our Lord's Tomb, and the Spirit is the source of new life. Clearly the people of God, divine in origin, is truly a people; built by the sacrifice of Christ and by the Spirit, it is truly an edifice; as the body of Christ, it is a true body. All this concerns an order of execution, of realization unfolding itself in certain structures. These structures are not left to chance or whim; they are given and established by Christ, priest, king and prophet, and animated by the life-giving Spirit. They never take away the nature proper to human life and human society, which is liberty. On the contrary, this liberty is affirmed in the new creature by the Spirit 'because the creation itself will be set free from its bondage to decay and obtain the glorious liberty of the children of God' (Rom. 8. 21).

The New Testament covers that period of history which extends from the Pasch of Christ, his redemptive mysteries, to his second coming. This time of the history of the People of God is the time of the Church. At the foundation of the Church are the twelve apostles – among them Peter – whose mission is to carry abroad the gospel, i.e. to carry abroad Jesus himself, continually present in their midst through the Holy Spirit.

There is then *belief* and *continuity*. But there is also freedom for God's intervention in that continuity. This appears in the New Testament itself. There are the twelve, but there is also the election of Paul, who is to make known his Gospel through the pillars of the Church. There are interventions of the Spirit, sometimes unexpected. At Pentecost the Spirit 'rushes in' (Acts 2.2). But even if the event of Pentecost is altogether singular and therefore foundational for the Church (cf. Acts 1.18) it is also true that the most decisive moments for the nascent Church are marked by the intervention of the Spirit, e.g. the case of Cornelius, when the Spirit falls on those who hear Peter's preaching even before they have been baptized (Acts 10. 44 ff.) – which enables Peter to justify the mission to the Gentiles (Acts 11. 15–17). Other passages of the Acts could be analysed on the same lines – Stephen's discourse (Acts 7), the baptism of the Ethiopian eunuch (Acts 8. 26–39), the conversion of Paul and his baptism by Ananias (Acts 9. 1–18).

There is some truth then in the thesis of Professor Leuba (*A la découverte de l'espace oecuménique*; Paris, Delachaux, 1967) on the presence in the Church of an 'institution' and an 'event'. There is continuity in an apostolic tradition which is the Gospel of Christ announced in the Spirit and lived in the Spirit until his second coming: then there is a 'structure' of the covenant in which the apostles are the twelve foundations: 'among their number he chose Peter. . . . Meanwhile, Christ Jesus Himself forever remains the chief cornerstone.'[3] But within this structure there is also the free intervention of the Spirit which diversifies ministries, missions, charismata, and Paul is sent to the Gentiles as Peter is to the Jews (cf. Gal. 2. 7–9); even if the Church of Corinth is a 'sick church' (Von Allmen), it witnesses none the less to a diversity of charismata which Paul does not call in question. There is then, alongside institutional structures, a liberty of the Spirit in the history of the Church. He chooses the man for a given mission. He disposes the succession of events and the sociological factors for the fulfilling of the Church's mission, e.g. that Paul accomplishes his mission in a prearranged area, the Roman empire, the *oikoumènè* of those days, the Greek-speaking world where the Jews are dispersed. In itself the Roman Empire does not form part of the 'structures' of the Church, any more than does the 'Greek culture' – the background of the New Testament – but these are contingent factors that the Spirit makes use of for the Gospel.

The dialectic 'freedom–authority' does not seem to me to

3. The Decree on Ecumenism, *Unitatis Redintegratio*, of the Second Vatican Council, Nr. 2.

enter into the theological aspect of the problem we are discussing. Or rather it arises only secondarily when we have seen that the covenant in Jesus Christ supposes structures and at the same time liberty in the Spirit. Authority itself is submitted to liberty. Otherwise it remains purely in the juridical order.

Some historical considerations

In what way did the Church of the first centuries conceive and realize the principle of liberty, allowing diversity within given structures? Did it admit, as legitimate, differences in the expression of the catholic faith, in its theological exploration? In a study on 'The differences compatible with unity in the tradition of the ancient church down to the 12th century'[4] Fr. Lanne, O.S.B., distinguishes three fields: diversity in unity in the field of liturgical and disciplinary usage; diversity in unity in the field of theological 'terminology'; diversity in unity in the field of theological 'systems'.

(1) Eusebius in his *Historia Ecclesiastica* (V, 23–5) tells of a grave dispute in the ancient Church over the paschal question. Pope Victor of Rome threatened to excommunicate the bishops of Asia who kept to the quartodeciman tradition, against the general usage of the Church. Irenaeus of Lyons, writing to Victor in the name of the bishops of Gaul on the question of the date of Easter and the practice of fasting, expresses a very different attitude.

The discussion is not only about the day, but also about the manner of fasting itself. Some in fact think they should fast for only one day, some for two, some for even longer. Some reckon forty hours of the day and night as their 'day'. And this variety of observance has not come about now, in our time, but goes back a long way to our ancestors who, without holding to absolute precision, as it seems, have preserved the custom in its simplicity and in its characteristic features and passed it on to us. They were all none the less anxious to preserve peace, and we should keep peace one with another. Difference in fasting confirms agreement in faith. (V, 25, 12–13; Lanne, op. cit. p. 229.)

In the same letter Irenaeus recalls the story of the encounter

4. D. Emmanuel Lanne, 'Les Différences compatibles avec l'unité dans la tradition de l'Eglise ancienne (jusqu'au XIIe siècle)', *Istina* 8 (1961–2), 227–53.

between Anicetus and Polycarp. They held to different observances in celebrating Easter. Anicetus could not convince Polycarp nor Polycarp Anicetus. But they kept communion with each other and Anicetus allowed Polycarp to celebrate the Eucharist in his church. Eusebius ends his chapter on the paschal question with this note on Irenaeus: 'Irenaeus did credit to his name – he was a peacemaker in name and in deed; in this fashion did he appeal for and bring about the peace of the Church.' (V, 23. 18; op. cit. p. 230.)

Socrates, the 'Scholastic' of Constantinople, the continuator of Eusebius's work and like him more of a historian than a theologian, has left us a series of examples which illustrate the liturgical and disciplinary divergences in the ancient Church. He gives details of the paschal dispute which was prolonged to the end of the fourth century in the Novatian church of Constantinople, the diversity in the observing of fasts, the variations in the days of synaxis, the differences between the several churches regarding clerical celibacy, varieties of usage in administering baptism, in orientating churches, in celebrating the Saturday vigil. He says: 'All in all, you would be hard put to it to find among all the communities in the world two churches which in every respect celebrate the liturgy in the same way.' (*Hist. Eccl.*, V. 22; P.G. 67 col. 632B.)

At the same time the differences are not arbitrary; each local church clings to its immemorial traditions. The varieties of usage do not argue any difference in matters of faith, or a severing of communion. The apostles, according to the writings of the New Testament, imposed in the Council of Jerusalem only what was strictly necessary, and allowed divergences in local practice.

In the west we have the witness of St. Augustine, theologian and pastor. For him the variety of local usage expresses the richness of the Church, spouse of Christ. As a theologian he acknowledges here a positive value; as a pastor he adds the principle that we should not harm the brethren who follow different usages. Apart from what is prescribed by Holy Scripture, apostolic tradition and the general councils, we should conform to the usage of the local church so as not to arouse vain disputes. He has in mind immemorial local traditions and he opposes innovations introduced by individuals, clerical or lay. The principle of charity, bond of unity, should govern legitimate differences between churches.[5] In all this St. Augustine follows the attitudes of St. Ambrose.

At Rome Popes Siricius (4th cent.) and Innocent I (5th cent.) show a contrary attitude. In liturgico-disciplinary practices all Western Churches should strictly follow the Roman usage. The argument is that all the Churches of the West were founded by the apostle Peter or by his successors. St. Ambrose and St. Augustine would not have adopted such an attitude (cf. Lanne, op. cit. p. 238).

Nevertheless this rigid line has not always prevailed at Rome. We have the example of Pope Gregory the Great in his replies to Augustine of Canterbury. Against the tendency towards a too narrow fidelity to Roman usages, the Pope here recognizes and guarantees to a local church the possibility of a liturgy of its own.[6]

After the patristic period, and above all since the twelfth century, liturgico-disciplinary centralization takes place around the two Christian capitals, Rome and Constantinople, and creates, above all in the West, the liturgical uniformity we know.

(2) More important perhaps than the field of liturgy and discipline is that of theology. Is there found at the origins of Christian theology, liberty of thought and expression within the communion of the same faith? Can we discern theological diversity in the profession of the common faith?

From the apostolic times the Church knew numerous heresies, and the attitude of the biblical writers as of early doctors of the Church was severe and uncompromising. All the same, when there is no question of the content of the faith but only of explanation or formulation of its mysteries, e.g. the Trinity or Christology, we find in Hilary, Athanasius, and Basil a spirit of comprehension and a conciliatory attitude which saved or restored peace in a very grave dispute. They demanded that the Nicene Faith should be confessed, that the Arian heresy and those which treated the Holy Spirit as a creature should be anathematized; but nothing more.

---

5. *Ep.* xxxvi to Casulanus; see Lanne op. cit. p. 233; cf. also *Epp.* liv and lv to Januarius; Lanne op. cit. pp. 234–7.

6. The Venerable Bede, *Hist. Eccl.* xxvii, 2; *P.L.* **95**, cols 58C–59A; Lanne op. cit. p. 239.

Were these theologians conscious of the theological implications of their 'economy', which really involves much more than a different terminology and leaves room for a different theological approach to the mysteries of faith? Whatever the answer, there are traces of this in the Creed of Constantinople (381) in which the divinity of the Holy Spirit is not expressed explicitly by the term *theos* as for the Father and the Son, but in equivalent terms: 'Qui cum Patre et Filio coadoratur (simul adoratur) et conglorificatur' ('Who is adored equally with the Father and the Son and equally glorified').

(3) Theological differences showed themselves more clearly in the Christological controversies between the schools of Alexandria and Antioch in the fifth century. Were the divergences of thought between Cyril of Alexandria and John of Antioch 'after all no more than ill-natured quarrels', as P. Th. Camelot puts it? [7] Without doubt the Acta of the Council of Ephesus include the third letter of Cyril to Nestorius with its twelve anathemas, but the same Acts do not say anything about their approval. [8] Yet after the Council, the opposition between the two theologies which had been face to face there remained irreducible (Camelot, op. cit. p. 71). In 433 John of Antioch, to restore peace, wrote to Cyril and sent him his confession of faith. In this letter he expresses all the Antiochene theology on the two natures of Christ, and even aims it explicitly against Cyril's 4th anathema, but he confesses no less clearly the unity of the person (prosôpon) and the divine motherhood of Mary. He accepts equally the deposition of Nestorius. [9]

Cyril replies with true magnanimity. He rejoices at the peace in the Church. 'Let the heavens rejoice and the earth be glad – the barriers of separations are cast down . . . all dissent is put aside' (*Ep.* 39; *P.G.* 77, 173–81) and he does not insist on the disputed expressions 'single nature', 'physical union', 'hypostasis'. (Cf. Camelot, op. cit. 72.)

As Fr. Lanne puts it, 'he accepted a profession of faith in

7. Cf. P. Th. Camelot, *Ephèse et Chalcédoine* (Histoire des Conciles Oecuméniques, Nr. 2; Ed. de l'Orante, Paris, 1961), p. 67.
8. Cf. Denz. Schönm., Note to Nr. 250 ff.; Camelot, op. cit. p. 67, and P. Gallier in *Rech. Sc. Rel.* 23 (1933), 45 ff., maintains that there was no approval; for the opposite opinion see Lanne, op. cit. p. 248.
9 Letter of John of Antioch to Cyril, in Correspondence of Cyril, *Ep.* 38: *P.G.* 77, 172–3.

which the theological perspective was not his own' (op. cit. p. 249). Pope Sixtus III congratulates both Cyril and John. The Council of Chalcedon later canonizes Cyril's letter, 'Disengaging from school controversies the common faith of the Church in the Incarnate Word and in the Theotokos'. (Camelot, op. cit. p. 72.)

The peace was insecure. The theologians of both Alexandria and Antioch tried after the Council (451) to impose their own exclusivist theology. In a study of 'Les Schismes à l'Epoque des Premiers Conciles' Charles Moeller comes to this conclusion about the sixth century: 'The Byzantine sixth century is of decisive importance for the history of the schisms which were to arise later. It teaches us a lesson valid for our time as well as for ancient times: that various theological schools must co-exist peacefully within the single tradition of the Faith. The unity of the Church is not to be confused with outward uniformity, no more than with the triumph of one theological school.' [10]

At the origins of Christianity we find a divergence which was to mark the situation of the Church for four centuries – that between the Judaeo-Christian Church (Ecclesia ex Judaeis) and the gentile Christian Church (Eccelesia ex gentibus). Archaeological discoveries, literature and monuments witness to the survival of Judaeo-Christian communities not merely in the second century but down to the sixth. Fr. Bagatti has given a first synthesis of the data in his recent book *L'Eglise de la Circoncision* (Jerusalem, Imprim. Française, 1965). It shows Jewish-Christian communities between the second and fifth centuries in Judaea, Samaria, Galilee, Transjordania and Syria. For Asia Minor, Egypt and Rome the problem remains whether such communities were Jewish-Christian in the strict sense or merely under Jewish-Christian influence. In a review of Fr. Bagatti's book, Fr. Daniélou describes these communities thus:

The essential of the Jewish-Christian communities is their fidelity to Jewish observances. They are Christians coming from Judaism, who have refused not only the position of Paul but even that of the Council of Jerusalem, and hence found themselves in a state of schism. For them, a Christian is a Jew who has come to believe

10. Published in *L'Eglise et les Eglises* (Chevetogne, 1954), 241–60; see p. 258.

in Christ without ceasing to be a Jew by observance. They are thus in a line of continuity with original Christianity.[11]

Here I put a question. Did the Jewish-Christian communities really find themselves in schism? The Council of Jerusalem, in the discourse of James and in the apostolic letter, decided not to lay upon the gentile brethren greater burdens than 'these necessary things' (cf. Acts 15.28 and 15.19). The Council in fact does not impose on the Hellenists the observances of the Jewish law, but these remain allowed and practised among the Jewish Christians. The Hellenic Christians were obliged to abstain from certain things simply in order that the Jewish Christians in consorting with them should not incur legal pollution. Thus communion of faith and charity could be maintained between two communities undoubtedly very different in their liturgical and disciplinary practices, in their spirituality and in their thinking about the relation between the Law and the Gospel. St. Paul describes this communion, this unity of two in one body (cf. Eph. 2.16). Literary sources and archaeological discoveries offer evidence that Jewish-Christian communities did not persevere in this unity of structure and communion of the New Covenant. It would be interesting to know how long this particular diversity in unity survived, and what was the theology, liturgy and discipline of these communities.

Professor H. Cazelles has studied the idea of the People of God in its Jewish and Christian contexts, trying to reconcile the two by an appreciation of the Torah as the gift of God, regarded by both communities as divinely inspired.[12] He concludes by relating the problem of Jewish–Christian divergence within the structure of the People of God to the Church's situation today:

Doctrinally speaking, if one sees in the Bible nothing more than conditions set by God for men to reach eternal happiness, then the two interpretations of the Torah, the Jewish and the Christian, appear at loggerheads as two opposite types of observance. But if one regards the Bible as bearing witness to God's creative action, calling for the faith of believers in the midst of the universe in

11. Cf. 'Bulletin d'histoire des origines chrétiennes'; *Rech. Sc. Rel.*, **55** (1967), pp. 88–103.
12. H. Cazelles, 'The People of God', in *Encounter Today*, **2** (1967), pp. 13–15.

order to 'purchase' (1 Pet. 2.9) a people for himself, then a symbio-
sis seems possible in view of St. Paul's principle, that 'the gifts and
the calling of God are irrevocable' (Rom. 11.29). Indeed the gift
of God made to mankind and of course to Israel (by the redeeming
action of the Word Incarnate, the heir to God and the heir to
David) does not cancel the gift of law: the Torah was not
abolished, as stated clearly by Matthew (5.17) and St. Paul (Rom.
3.31) though to anyone who has met Christ in his Church it is
obvious that the Torah does not bring us what we receive from
Christ.

This theology should condition our practical attitudes on
both sides:

A Christian should regard the structure of the People of God
living under the Law as legitimate and acceptable to God who
gave them the Torah. . . . But the Christian should beware of
ascribing to the Law what it does not claim to give: the Law is a
precondition for salvation and a pedagogue (or schoolmaster)
(Gal. 3.24): it does not possess the same power for grace and salvation as the Christian finds in Christ. . . .
So, as regards the Jew, it would seem right for him to follow
the example of Rabbi Gamaliel (cf. Acts 5.34–39) who took the
defence of the early Christians in Jerusalem against the Sadducees,
and admit the existence of a Jewish-Christian Church in the sense
of the Church of St. James, which was fully faithful to Jewish
observance, temple worship, fasting and vows, and at the same
time fully believing in Jesus Christ. However, a revival in some
shape or other of the Church of St. James would be at the present
moment unthinkable; in the first place because the Vatican Council has not yet borne all its fruits among Christians and secondly
because there is too much anti-Christian resentment among Jews.
(Cazelles, op. cit. pp. 12–13.)

In a note Prof. Cazelles adds:

The Jewish world would no doubt consider such a restoration [of
the Church of St. James] as a subtle form of proselytism and many
Christians would regard it almost as a form of apostasy if a
Christian of Jewish descent had his son circumcised – which to
my mind woud be quite normal. (op. cit. p. 13.)

The present problem

History then shows that not merely liturgical and disciplinary differences but also those of terminology and even of
theology are found at the ecclesial level itself, within the
reality of the local Church. They are found within a unity of
faith, of sacramental life, of structure.

The Second Vatican Council has recognized and emphasized the legitimate differences which have existed *ab origine* between the Churches of East and West. The Council did not merely describe the differences as they exist in fact, but in the historical spirit traced them to their source, which reveals the reason for them and sets them in a total context, which is that of the local Church. Between local Churches there should be fraternal relations in the communion of faith and charity, as between sister-churches, and this within the perfect communion of all with the apostolic see of Rome, which is at the same time the visible sign of communion between all the local Churches.

This reality of the local Church is one of the fundamental notions of Vatican II, which sets out the doctrinal basis of it in *Lumen Gentium* (Nr. 23–7) in the Constitution on the Liturgy (Nr. 41), in the Decree *Christus Dominus* on the Bishop's Pastoral Office in the Church (Nr. 11), in the Decree *Ad Gentes* on the Church's Missionary Activity (Nr. 18–20) and in the Decree *Unitatis Redintegratio* on Ecumenism (Nr. 14–17).

If early church history necessarily presents to us the local Church mainly as coterminous with the city-state of late antiquity, we should not suppose that the Council is being unrealistic and antiquarian and merely looking backwards to these precedents. Historical precedents can give us some guidance in the present search for unity -- in our approach to contemporary pluralism which is of many and diverse kinds. Today a single diocese, even a single parish, can embrace a bewildering variety of races, beliefs, social traditions etc., but equally the religious tradition of, say, a country or group of countries can be a powerful and complex unifying force, not always on the conscious level.

If we understand the reality of the local Church merely as a somewhat superficial difference of liturgical and disciplinary forms within a unity and uniformity of spiritual life and theological vision, we shall certainly not grasp the richness and depth of its ecclesial life. This is the criticism of the too juridical and disciplinary conception of the Eastern Churches which has developed among us Roman Catholics; it has perhaps developed equally in the Anglican and Lutheran Churches at times with regard to those ritualist tendencies which borrow liturgical forms from Rome. The notion of 'rite' simply does not explain the full reality of a local Church unless indeed it be understood as embracing everything in that Church which is essential and vital: its own proper way of embodying the preaching of the Gospel and the celebration of worship and sacraments in a determined local community in communion with other local Churches. This truly implies a liturgy, a discipline, a spirituality and a theology which are proper to it.

The local Church is a 'portion of the People of God' (*Christus Dominus*, Nr. 11), having all the gifts of grace by which the Church, a chosen people, is built and grows (*Unitatis Redintegratio*, Nr. 15). As people of God it is a people 'rooted in social life and considerably adapted to the local culture' (*Ad Gentes*, Nr. 19) where mystical riches are dispensed and find expression 'in a manner harmonious with the nature and the genius of each nation' (ibid. Nr. 18). These are highly significant expressions, stressing the genuine and positive elements that can exist in national tradition. It is thus that, at the beginning of this paper, we have conceived the People of God as made up of a multitude of peoples. The Vatican Council has well disclosed the manifold richness in the structure of the unique and universal Church in conceiving the episcopal structure as collegial and in establishing episcopal conferences. It is thus that within the framework of a universal structure there has been achieved freedom for the proper development of local Churches.

Can theological considerations about the nature of the People of God, together with the lessons of history, guide us in solving the problems set by the present situation of a divided Christianity?

We are confronted with what Paul VI has called 'pluralism which extends to essentials and is therefore intolerable'.[13] We have lived disunited for centuries. We have created doctrines which have not remained within the communion of faith and charity but have broken it. Christianity no longer manifests the varied richness of a communion of sister-churches – it presents to the world 'incomprehensible sectarian exclusiveness' (Paul VI. loc. cit. 497).

13. Speech of 28 April 1967 to the Secretariat for Promoting Christian Unity, *Act. Ap. Sed.* 59 (1967), 493–512.

Yet, along with this very significant consideration, we have seen the relevance of sixth-century Byzantium to our own situation – unity is not uniformity now any more than it was then, and diversity may well become richer within a more striking and edifying unity. A deeper understanding of ancient history and of our own situation may reinforce each other: providing we are not siding with Cyril or John to reinforce our own prejudices, they may both guide us to find our way to peace out of a seeming impasse without forsaking either steadfastness or magnanimity.

Whatever the situation, all Christian dialogue presupposes a certain measure of communion. The *dialogue of charity*, which is much more than a relation of courtesy and friendship, will bring us to recognize and accept legitimate and authentically Christian differences which have developed during the centuries of separation, in the spirit of Cyril and John. The *dialogue of truth* will unite us in the mystery of faith, worship and sacraments. If we say that there will be tension, or rather dialectic, between structure and liberty – both of them given and guaranteed by our Lord Jesus Christ – this is not a form of words to slide round our difficulties, but a reminder to maintain our perspective in facing them.

'All are led to examine their own faithfulness to Christ's will for the Church and, wherever necessary, undertake with vigor the task of renewal and reform' (*Unitatis Redintegratio*, Nr. 4). Now, Christ did not will the schisms and ruptures which we have dragged on with for so many centuries. But he did will diversity within communion. Is it not a sign of new development that in 1967 we celebrate at Rome the centenary of the martyrdom of the two apostles Peter and Paul, whereas in 1867 only the martyrdom of St. Peter was commemorated? This diversity of local Churches within a unity has been the great theme of the messages and speeches of Pope and Ecumenical Patriarch since the recent meeting in Constantinople. Dialogue is not enough. To renew oneself, to reform oneself means to sacrifice oneself. 'To find ourselves one in diversity and in fidelity', said the Pope at Constantinople 'can only be the work of the Spirit of love.' [14]

14. Talk of 27 July 1967, *Act. Ap. Sed.* **59** (1967), p. 841.

6

Unity and Comprehensiveness

A PAPER PRESENTED AT HUNTERCOMBE,
1 SEPTEMBER 1967

BISHOP J. R. H. MOORMAN and

PROFESSOR HOWARD E. ROOT

According to the minutes of the Gazzada meeting the scope of this paper (No. 7) was to be as follows: 'To what extent can or should there be diversity in a united church? Freedom and authority.' Our recollection, however, is that the word 'comprehensiveness' played a large part in the discussion and that at least part of our brief was to give some account of this notion, both in theory and in practice. We felt however that in this context the problem of comprehensiveness is virtually indistinguishable from that of diversity in (or within) unity. In this paper we shall move from more or less general and abstract principles to the more specific cases where, at least *prima facie*, there would seem to be divergence between Anglican and Roman Catholic understanding of the limits of permissible diversity, or the extent of desirable comprehensiveness.

We can begin with some almost platitudinous observations about which, we take it, there is no Anglican/Roman Catholic controversy. When we speak of unity, the restoration of full unity between Rome and Canterbury of which we spoke in our Gazzada communiqué, we are not thinking merely of administrative and juridical re-arrangements which would bring practical benefits. Christian unity is sometimes argued for in terms which are largely pragmatic. And the models of a reunited church which are put before us sometimes owe more to the worlds of politics and commerce than to the Gospel. (Cf. Professor Ian Henderson's recent attack on Anglicanism in terms of political 'conspiracy' and 'imperialism'.) Of course there are good practical, economic, administrative reasons for the reunion of separated Churches, but in themselves they are neither the ground nor the justification for ecumenical hope. The only unity worth having is unity in truth, and the hope for its achievement rests not upon the skill of ecclesiastical negotiations but upon the agreed theological datum that unity is God's will.

One could elaborate upon this at length, but it is necessary to say at least this much in order to establish some kind of background for a discussion of diversity, or diversity *in* unity. We are not interested in that kind of unity which would be based on a series of lowest common denominators in belief and practice. Because we take unity more seriously we must leave no doubt in anyone's mind that a collection of diversities, given a new name, would be no realization of unity. A merely permissive attitude to diversity would fail to do justice to the theological ground of unity. In this context there can be no proper analogy between the Church and the permissive, liberal-democratic state. Such a state can afford a wide margin of tolerance in, say, matters of political, moral or religious opinion. So long as the rights of others are not interfered with, and accepted standards of behaviour not flagrantly broken or mocked, anything goes. You may even, as a matter of right, hold quite outrageous opinions. But unless you try to force them on others or shout them from the housetops, the state will not busy itself to correct you.

If it were thought that this political situation offered an analogy for a reunited Church, extraordinary things would follow. All opinions and beliefs would be permissible; or, to put it the other way, none would be obligatory. It would be as though the Church were saying, 'For the sake of unity – or for the sake of giving the impression of unity to the outside world – we will all observe certain outward rules. But privately, of course, you can believe as you please or not believe at all.'

As against any such point of view we should want to argue – perhaps at first sight paradoxically – that any merely permissive attitude to diversity fails and must be ruled out not because it is heedless of real unity but because it does not take diversity itself seriously enough. To explain this, we shall have to look more closely at what we mean by rightful (or even necessary) diversity in the Church. It is now a commonplace to accept this rightfulness. Few voices are raised in favour of rigid uniformity; in fact everyone takes pains to emphasize that unity and uniformity are very different things. The fact of diversity, then, which has sometimes been condemned and sometimes feared, has become theologically respectable. But if this new respectability is more than pragmatism or an adjustment compelled by a pluralistic society, we shall have to be confident in its theological underpinning.

No one needs to be told that diversity, or comprehensiveness, is not only a significant but a central part of Anglican tradition. Historically, of course, this tradition owes much to the vicissitudes of the English Church in the sixteenth and seventeenth centuries. But Anglican divines, then and since, have maintained that this tradition is not merely something which historical circumstances forced upon the Church. They have, to the contrary, claimed that comprehensiveness is a necessary quality in any Church which pretends to catholicity, that it is in this sense a mark of the Church and that its absence turns church into sect. But at the same time none would deny that the ideal of diversity in unity creates problems and tensions, both theological and practical. One of these, for us, especially since the beginnings of the ecumenical movement, is the problem of explaining the Anglican position to our separated Christian brethren. To the non-Anglican that position sometimes looks like no position at all. Yet perhaps at the same time it has held a certain fascination, for the Anglican quest did not begin and end in England, and today the Provinces of Canterbury and York form but a small minority of the world-wide Anglican Communion of autonomous Churches in communion with the See of Canterbury.

One aspect of the non-Anglican's puzzlement was brought out in a recent interview which the Archbishop of Canterbury gave for Italian Television:

Question: 'Your Grace, what exactly is the distinction between High Church and Low Church?'
The Archbishop of Canterbury: 'Our Church of England has two aspects. On the one hand we claim to be a Church possessing Catholic tradition and continuity from the ancient Church, and our Catholic tradition and continuity includes the belief in the

Real Presence of Christ in the Blessed Sacrament, the order of Episcopacy and the Priesthood, including the power of priestly absolution; these are parts of the Catholic continuity as we have it. We also possess various institutions belonging to Catholic Christendom, like monastic orders for men and women. That aspect of Catholic sacramental life and continuity is especially emphasized and cherished by people called High Church.

Our Anglican tradition has another aspect as well. We are a Church which has been through the Reformation and values many experiences derived from the Reformation, for instance the Open Bible; great importance is attached to the authority of the Holy Scriptures, and to personal conviction and conversion through the work of the Holy Spirit, and that aspect of our church life – the aspect connected with the reformation, the Open Bible and the personal conviction and conversion – is cherished specially by people sometimes called Low Church.

'But I want to emphasize that though there is High Church and Low Church, it is all the time *one* Church with a single life, and all the members of our Church share together in the Creeds, Holy Scriptures, the Sacraments, the rule of the Bishops and the liturgy; so do not think of High Church and Low Church as utterly separate factions, but as two aspects of the life of a Church which is all the time one.'

The Archbishop does not here use the word comprehensiveness, but the idea of diversity in unity is what he is talking about and the way he approaches his answer to the question is very typically Anglican.

Before we look further at the theological questions, this is perhaps the place to record Anglican fascination with recent Roman Catholic emphasis upon the rightfulness of diversity within the Church. Quite apart from the diversities of approach which so many Roman Catholic theologians have manifested since the Council, we think in particular of utterances by Pope John and Pope Paul and of passages in the decrees of the Council. It may be useful to cite several of these in the hope that our discussions might profit from close attention to them.

We would suspect that a most important keynote was struck by Pope John's allocution at the opening of the Council. After stressing the fact that the Council was not convened to define 'new' doctrines, or to adjudicate between varying theological opinions, or simply to reiterate traditional teaching, he went on to say,

The whole world expects a step forward toward a doctrinal pene-
tration and a formation of consciousness in faithful and perfect
conformity to the authentic doctrine, which, however, should be
studied and expounded through the methods of research and
through the literary forms of modern thought. The substance of
the ancient doctrine of the deposit of faith is one thing, and the
way in which it is presented is another.

This latter sentence is often quoted and would seem to provide the charter for a liberality and diversity in theological
interpretation. Certainly that diversity was marked and un-
hampered in the actual proceedings of the Council.

The same theme was part of Pope Paul's allocution at the
opening of the Second Session. In speaking of his hopes for
the restoration of Christian unity he said that this

visible union cannot be attained except in identity of faith and by
participation in the same sacraments and in the organic harmony
of a single ecclesiastical control, even though this allows for a great
variety of verbal expressions, movements, lawful institutions, and
preferences with regard to modes of acting.

This allowance and recognition of variety recurred in his
allocution at the opening of the Third Session when, after
speaking of 'the long, sad history which led up to the various
separations' he went on to 'recall the words of the Apostle
Paul, who brought the gift of the Gospel to all nations, seeking
to become all things to all men. Such an adaptability as we
might today be tempted to call pluralism in practice . . .'
'Pluralism in practice' would seem a very apt motto for a united
Church which wished to allow for diversity in unity.

A number of the decrees of the Council give further embodiment to these principles, but we recall especially some passages
in the decree *On Ecumenism*. For example in No. 4 it is said,

While preserving unity in essentials, let all members of the Church,
according to the office entrusted to each, preserve a proper freedom in the various forms of spiritual life and discipline, in the
variety of liturgical rites, and even in the theological elaboration
of revealed truth. In all things let charity be exercised.

The same point is made, even more forcibly, in the section of
the decree dealing with the Orthodox Churches of the East,
and is reinforced by passages in the recently published *Direc-
torium* on Ecumenism. In one sense, of course, we realize that

this recognition of rightful diversity in the Eastern Churches (i.e. diversity from many Latin rules and practices) is no new thing. But it would seem to make more public and prominent a certain comprehensiveness which already belongs to the Roman Catholic Church.

Finally, in the decree *On Ecumenism* (No. 11) there is an interesting passage which seems to bear upon any Roman Catholic attitude to diversities of Christian attitude and expression within the whole body of Christian Churches and Communities. 'When comparing doctrines, they [theologians] should remember that in Catholic teaching there exists an order or "hierarchy" of truths, since they vary in their relationship to the foundation of the Christian faith.' This notion of a hierarchy of truths, when taken in conjunction with the other pronouncements we have mentioned, would seem to encourage that kind of dialogue which could only proceed fruitfully if a certain theological diversity were not only recognized but welcomed.

No doubt these quotations are all patient of more than one interpretation – like many Anglican pronouncements – but we have felt it worthwhile to cite them here as a basis for discussion. If there is a Roman Catholic uncertainty about the definition of Anglican diversity, there is now also an Anglican uncertainty about the interpretation and repercussions of recent Roman Catholic utterances. It is our feeling that new developments have brought our positions nearer together, but only further dialogue will show the extent of the agreement and disagreement which will now be our starting point.

We can now return to the more general theological considerations which seem to us fundamental in any search for the justification of diversity or comprehensiveness in the Church. We have said that any merely pragmatic or indifferentist attitude to diversity fails because it does not really take diversity seriously. In our view the place for diversity within the unity of the Church is dictated not by exigencies of history or the convenience of ecclesiastical organization, but by the mystery of Christian faith itself. It is a constant Biblical as well as patristic theme that God is not only beyond our powers of comprehension but also beyond any words which human beings, in theological and doctrinal formulations, can

find to express their understanding of His nature and will.
(Compare, for example, St. Hilary of Poitiers on the Arian
struggle and the Council of Nicaea.) It would seem to follow
from this that in the Church there must always be allowance
for a diversity of words and images used and tried for evoking
something of the fullness of that mystery. Fullness of expression is beyond us, but in any age (and perhaps in our own most
notably) there is the need for diversity in expression. At times
this diversity may become so great that the very unity of the
faith seems to be threatened. This will always be a danger
(as it was felt to be in the early Church when St. Paul insisted
upon the rightfulness of his Gentile mission), but history
would seem to show that tensions and struggles are necessary
if anything like the fullness of the faith is to be evoked and
communicated. The very imagery of the One Body – as St.
Paul understood it – requires a diversity not only of gifts but
of expressions. If we understand revelation as active, dynamic,
and personal, we shall also understand it as taking place within
the continuing human circumstances of struggle and dialogue.

The importance of diversity is, as it were, both horizontal
and vertical. In any particular age more than one set of words
and images is necessary if Christian truth is to transcend cultural differences. Similarly, in ages separated by time and
circumstance there is bound to be variety and divergence in
expression and understanding. Otherwise the Church will be
in danger of lapsing into what Michael Novak aptly called
'non-historical orthodoxy'. It is our impression that, following
Fr. Schillebeeckx, the fundamental 'battle of mind' witnessed
by the Council lay precisely here. The very dynamism and
inner life of Christian faith depends upon development, and
that means the recognition of the need for diversity, at any
time, in theological method and exploration. (In this connection we find interesting Pope Paul's recent 're-instatement'
of Duns Scotus. It might be said that this was only the encouragement of diversity in philosophy, but we doubt whether
one can really draw so neat a line between philosophy and
theology. The acceptance of certain philosophical and meta-
physical modes to a great extent determines theological attitudes and expressions.) We should also want to claim that what
is true about the place of diversity in theology proper also

applies in other aspects of the Church's life: worship, discipline, etc.

But having recognized the essential character of diversity we are not unaware of the problems it creates. These would seem to pose the fundamental theological problems for the discussion. How are we to keep diversities in balance with the demand for unity in truth and faith? We will not even attempt any general answer to this question, but we see two sorts of problems which should occupy a central place in dialogue. The first are more theoretical. How is essential *continuity* in faith to be understood and guaranteed? Can this be rightly confined to verbal and juridical categories? Given the continual need for theological *development*, what are to be the criteria for distinguishing between legitimate and illegitimate development in doctrine, belief and practice? Traditionally it has of course been allowed that on many matters there may be varieties of theological opinion. But this has been balanced by the insistence that such variety is not permissible in matters of 'defined' doctrine. We find this less simple than it looks, for there are always problems about the *meaning* of definitions, so that we find it hard to understand how definitions can be considered static and, as it were, self-explanatory. The history of Christian doctrine would seem to show that there has been no less controversy about the rightful interpretation of certain definitions than about doctrines undefined (e.g. Atonement). Once again it is problems about method and criteria of interpretation which need closest attention. Definition as such does not foreclose discussion. (Do we 'understand' the Chalcedonian definition precisely as the fathers of Chalcedon understood it? Or did ever all of them understand it in exactly the same way? Did all of the fathers of Vatican II understand 'collegiality' in precisely the same way?)

The second sort of problems (while by no means untheological) have more to do with the practical needs of the Church in the world. Here we are thinking of two contrasted but complementary needs. Many Anglicans would insist no less than Roman Catholics on the need for a focus and centre of authority in the visible Church – pastoral in purpose and intention, but also unavoidably juridical. We should even want to say that the more diversity was cherished, the greater the need for such a centre and focus. Some Christian communities, because of their distaste for any diversity in their body, perhaps have less sense of need for such a focus. Their unity is defined by a kind of strict uniformity and identity, and to express any diversity would simply be to leave the body. But in a re-united Church which not only allowed but welcomed diversity, the need for some kind of visible focus would seem to us clear. This of course leads into highly controversial questions, and at the moment (to take only three examples) Roman Catholic, Orthodox and Anglican views on the nature and scope of this visible centre obviously diverge. There are signs that we are coming closer together here, but lengthy discussion and dialogue is essential.

The complementary need is for a great freedom and flexibility in the structures of the Church so that it can always be responsive to the movements of the Spirit. Here there are many varieties in Anglican thinking (and perhaps also in Roman Catholic thinking). But we should be inclined to say that, as in the political order, freedom and flexibility can only be maintained within a settled structure of authority.

As dialogue proceeds we may all be in for surprises on the way to restoration of unity. Those who are most concerned to defend rightful diversity may find that only within an accepted visible unity can diversity be developed and defended against sectarian tyrannies. Those most concerned with a visible authority and unity may find that without the acceptance of diversity, unity shrivels into narrow sectarianism and denies itself the power of growth and development.

These then are some of the fundamental issues, as we see them, for profitable dialogue on unity and comprehensiveness. We have not taken our brief to extend to any detailed discussion of particular doctrinal and other issues which appear to separate Anglican and Roman Catholic positions. But perhaps we can mention some of these, in the hope that our discussion may help to clarify Anglican minds on Roman Catholic attitudes about the rightfulness and limits of diversity, i.e. of comprehensiveness within the Church. In our Gazzada discussions several issues were brought out: Mariological, liturgical, devotional, and moral. On these issues we should like to put questions about what the Roman Catholic Church might insist upon in any re-united Church. In Mariology, for example, what are the limits of diversity, say, in interpretations of the dogma of the Assumption? In devotion, how are Anglicans to distinguish between practices which Roman Catholics consider essential to Christian faith and those which, however valuable in certain contexts, are not considered essential? In liturgical practice, how far is experimentation and variety to be encouraged and at precisely what points is it denied?

Moral questions deserve far more attention that we can give them here, but our feeling is that these may become increasingly important as dialogue develops. As we see it, there are three areas. First, and uncontroversially, there are many moral questions on which we have no fundamental disagreement, any more than any Christians. Second, there are questions upon which we both allow legitimate divergence of conscience, e.g. pacifism. Third, the questions on which we diverge fundamentally, e.g. birth control. As we see it, reunion will perhaps encounter as many problems in the moral sphere as in the purely theological one. For example, we cannot conceive of a situation in which – in a re-united Church – the Anglican position on birth control was denied.

At this juncture we deliberately leave out of account two very important questions. Mixed marriages, we agreed at Gazzada, should be referred to a special and separate commission. Clerical celibacy, which we regard as a matter of local discipline, has perhaps taken a new turn in the light of the most recent papal pronouncement. But we assume that this remains a matter of discipline. In any case, the Anglican position is known to us all. But how far, in the West, can the Roman Catholic Church meet the Anglican position if we are to move forward to a restoration of unity? In one sense this is a very secondary question, but in practical and public terms it is very important.

Finally, we think we can express the deep appreciation of Anglicans at the moves towards 'comprehensiveness' which the Roman Catholic Church has evidenced in and through Vatican II. In this paper we have tried to point to general principles and practical problems, only in the hope that our discussions will aid to clarity on both sides.

7

Unity: An Approach by Stages?

A PAPER PRESENTED AT MALTA,

DECEMBER/JANUARY 1967/8

BISHOP HENRY R. McADOO

Introduction

The Commission, at its meeting in Huntercombe Manor, gave us in general terms the task of drawing up, for discussion at the next meeting, an outline of what might be termed staged engagement or phased *rapprochement* between the Roman Catholic Church and the Anglican Communion, with the ultimate objective of organic unity.

The fact that the Preparatory Commission has been set up is an historic event, and an unprecedented one in the history of our two Churches. It was clearly the thinking of the Commission that unprecedented situations require unprecedented treatment. With this in mind, it appeared that the idea of growing together by stages should be examined, each stage being one which would be theologically justifiable.

The point of departure for such a joint theological investigation and the basis of the concept of phased *rapprochement* may well be claimed to be a sentence from the Common Declaration of the Pope and the Archbishop in March 1966: 'They intend to inaugurate between the Roman Catholic Church and the Anglican Communion a serious dialogue which, founded on the Gospels and on the ancient common traditions, may lead to that unity in truth, for which Christ prayed.'

From the Anglican point of view, such a basis is a welcome one, for Anglicans have always held themselves committed to 'the faith once for all delivered'. There is no such thing as the Anglican faith – only the faith, taught by Anglicans.

Andrewes formulated this more than three centuries ago, and it remains the basis: 'one canon . . . two testaments, three creeds, four general councils, five centuries, and the series of Fathers in that period . . . determine the boundary of our faith' (*Opuscula*, Library of Anglo-Catholic Theology ed., p. 91). Elsewhere, he wrote, referring to the definition of Vincent of Lérins: 'Let that be reckoned Catholic which always obtained everywhere among all, and which always and everywhere and by all was believed.' (*Responsio, ad Apologiam Cardinalis Bellarmini*, p. 25).

Laud, in his *Conference*, develops this in detail and by way of conclusion he writes:

> . . . and if the Scripture be the foundation to which we are to go for witness, if there be doubt about the faith, and in which we are to find the thing that is to be believed, as necessary in the faith; we never did, nor never will refuse any tradition that is universal and apostolic for the better exposition of the Scriptures; nor any definition of the Church in which she goes to the Scripture for what she teaches; and thrusts nothing as fundamental in the faith upon the world, but what the Scripture fundamentally makes '*materiam credendorum*', the substance of that which is so to be believed, whether immediately and expressly in words, or more remotely, where a clear and full deduction draws it out.

This sort of thing could be multiplied almost indefinitely from writings of the classical Anglican period, for Anglican theological method has consistently adhered to a three-fold appeal to Scripture, to antiquity, and to reason. It is important to note it, however, because it emphasizes how much Anglicans and Roman Catholics are agreed in accepting the historic faith. Divergences are not found here, but in the problems surrounding the question of the nature of authority and particularly as these impinge on the interpretation of the historic faith of the creeds, to which both our Churches are committed. This has constantly come to the surface hitherto in discussion, tending to crystallize around questions of papal infallibility and the *magisterium* of the teaching Church.

But it seems no more than a factual statement that Anglicans and Roman Catholics should be able to move forward from an accepted basis of the Gospels and the ancient common traditions.

The Lambeth Quadrilateral (Holy Scriptures, Creeds, the

sacraments of Baptism and Holy Communion, the apostolic ministry) emphasizes that the same position is held today, underlining as it does the given-ness of the faith and order of the Church. Again, both Churches recognize that the ministry has taken a three-fold form.

Both Churches are committed to preaching Christ, the Incarnate Word, and growth in fellowship with Him in the life of His Mystical Body: to proclaiming to the world the message of redemption and salvation as giving purpose and meaning to life in terms of man's supernatural end: to showing that the life which Christians live is 'the life which Christ lives in [them]'. (Gal. 2.20.) Both Churches see in the ministry of the Word and Sacraments the covenanted means of grace, the means by which men are 'built, as living stones,into a spiritual temple' (I Pet. 2.5). Given this, and since charity is the norm of action and dialogue, what stages can be visualized in the process of growing together?

Such stages should each in themselves be theologically justifiable, so that what is being sought is a series of steps theologically and practically feasible, which could be officially taken by the ecclesiastical authorities of both Churches.

Stage I

What kind of picture of the first stage could emerge from this approach to our present situation?

The first stage might well be one which would be inaugurated by taking two steps, one in the theological area and the other on the day-to-day level of Church life. It is well to remember that there is amongst members of both our Communions a diffused longing for unity which is complicated and partly vitiated by a certain amount of mutual distrust, the legacy of the past. It follows that all specific obstacles which block the growth of truly fraternal relations at the parochial level should be removed during this first stage. Otherwise, there would result merely a *rapprochement* of theologians.

The theological and practical steps must therefore be regarded as part of one operation, as necessarily complementary elements of Stage I in the coming together of the Roman Catholic Church and the Anglican Communion.

A

The theological step would be the recognition by both Churches that 'each believes the other to hold all the essentials of the Christian Faith'. Such recognition would 'not require from either communion the acceptance of all doctrinal opinion, sacramental devotion, or liturgical practice characteristic of the other'.

The quotations are from the Bonn Agreement (1931) between the Church of England and the Old Catholic Churches,[1] *and are given simply as an indication of the sort of line that might now be considered.* The common ground in that Agreement was fundamentals (see Introduction, above) in that the Declaration of Utrecht (1889), like Anglicanism, is committed to 'the Rule of Faith laid down by St. Vincent of Lérins' (*Decl.* 1).

The recent meeting between Pope Paul and Patriarch Athenagoras produced a declaration to the effect that each Church regarded the other as holding the fundamentals of the Catholic Faith, but neither was committed to the whole theological position of the other. At Huntercombe, a Roman Catholic speaker asked 'Why cannot we agree on fundamentals, and not insist on each other accepting all developments of doctrine?'

This would be the theological step in Stage I and something more can be said presently about its feasibility and about trends which might indicate it as a real possibility.

B

The practical step is really a complex of movements, but it might be summed up as the clearing away of obstacles to ecumenism on the parochial level – the level of the Church's life. Here again, the joint declaration of 24 March 1966 gave a clear pointer, indicating that dialogue should cover 'not only theological matters such as Scripture, tradition and liturgy, but also matters of practical difficulty, felt on either side'.

Experience shows that, if this aspect is not tackled simultaneously with the theological one, and the tangle of obstacles

1. Text in H. Bettenson (ed.), *Documents of the Christian Church*, Sect. XIV, III (paperback ed. 1967, p. 330). See also below, p. 95.

to charity and fraternity removed, the only growing-together
will be among delegates to theological conferences. Some of
the particular difficulties can be indicated later.

A

As to the theological step envisaged, what indications are
there that it might be acceptable to both Churches, and therefore a feasible step? On the Anglican side, the Articles with
their insistence on the doctrinal centrality of Scripture and
Creeds, the Lambeth Quadrilateral, and the form of the Bonn
Agreement, would all appear to indicate that such a step would
in fact be acceptable.

In consequence of this position, there is a built-in distinction in Anglican theology between fundamental and acces-
sory truths. This is quite explicit, and it is a constantly
recurring factor. So Henry Hammond distinguished 'between
theological verity and Catholic faith', the former including
things which are believed to be true but are not a necessary
part of fundamentals.[2] In fact, the whole drift of the classical
Anglican appeal to antiquity – which had nothing to do with
ecclesiastical antiquarianism – was, as Jeremy Taylor put it, in
respect of 'fundamentals and the rule of faith'. Paul Elmer
More's comment is to the point: 'To the Anglican the value
of tradition was measured by its tenacity of the original
depositum fidei.'[3] Taylor put it that 'when the Fathers appeal
to Tradition . . . it is such a tradition as delivers the fundamental points of Christianity, which were also recorded in
Scripture'.[4] In this book, Taylor looks at the doctrinal differences of Christians and examines the questions which are
still under discussion today, namely, the basis of authority in
the interpretation and declaration of the Faith. It is surpris-
ingly modern, dealing with the subjective approach, tradition,
infallibility and the place of reason in this situation. He pleads
for a coming together on fundamentals, and his book is far
from being naïve: 'If this consideration does not deceive me,
we have no other help in the midst of these distractions, and

2. *Works*, vol, i, p. 403.
3. P. E. More and F. L. Cross (edd.), *Anglicanism* (London, 1935), p. xxvi.
4. Jeremy Taylor, *The Liberty of Prophesying*, § v.

disunion, but all of us to be united in that common term, which as it does constitute the Church in its being such, so it is the medium of the communion of saints, and that is the Creed of the Apostles, and in all other things an honest endeavour to find out what truths we can, and a charitable and mutual permission to others that disagree from us and our opinions.[5]

It is the traditional Anglican distinction between fundamentals and accessories and theological opinions. It runs through all Anglican writings of the 17th century, such as Sanderson's *Pax Ecclesiae*, and it has nothing to do with minimalism or indifferentism. Its primary concern is with the unchangingness of fundamentals, the absolute necessity of these, and the difference between fundamentals and all else.

This is so much a part of Anglican teaching and thinking that it is hardly worth adducing further examples. Yet the views of Bramhall are very much to the point of the present subject, for he writes in terms of Christian unity. Bramhall sees the possibility of unity in returning to the position of the undivided Church when the creed was the foundation of the rule of faith, 'if the creed or necessary points of faith were reduced to what they were in the time of the four first oecumenical councils, according to the decree of the third general council'. Who, he asks, could say that 'the faith of the primitive fathers was insufficient'?

His analysis of Catholicity bears on the whole question of the feasibility of the step in Stage I which is under discussion. 'The communion of the Catholic Church' he writes 'is partly internal, partly external.' The former consists chiefly in acceptance of 'the same entire substance of saving necessary truth revealed by the apostles', in judgments of mutual charity, in the desire to achieve external communion, and in refusal to exclude those 'which profess the ancient faith of the apostles and primitive fathers, established in the first general councils, and comprehended in the Apostolic, Nicene and Athanasian creeds'. External communion consists in having the same creeds, sacraments, liturgy, and in accepting the same 'authority, that is, episcopacy or a general council'. Internal communion is a mutual obligation for all, even in the case of those with

5. ibid., Epistle Dedicatory.

whom external communion, for some reason, is not possible.

Catholicity derives 'by the uninterrupted line of apostolical succession' and depends on acceptance of the 'Scripture . . . that infallible rule', and on the acceptance of the unanimous and universal practice of the Church. It precludes 'censuring others of different judgement . . . in inferior questions' and 'obtruding opinions on others as articles of faith'. Bramhall's favourable view of the Eastern Churches was based on the fact that 'they exact of no man . . . any other creed', and the unity of Christians of the first centuries was founded on the fact that 'no Church exacted more in point of faith than the primitive creed'.[6]

The relevance of this apparent digression to the question of the theological feasibility of the suggested step in Stage I is that, on their formularies and on their past or recent statements and actions (as in the Bonn Agreement), Anglicans ought to be prepared to welcome such a proposal.

Is this distinction between fundamentals and secondary matters so very dissimilar to the concept of a hierarchy of truths which finds expression in the Vatican Council's Decree on Ecumenism?

C. II, xi, reads: 'Furthermore, Catholic theologians engaged in ecumenical dialogue, while standing fast by the teaching of the Church and searching together with separated brethren into the divine mysteries, should act with love for truth, with charity and with humility. When comparing doctrines, they should remember that in Catholic teaching there exists an order or "hierarchy" of truths, since they vary in their relationship to the foundation of the Christian faith.'

C. I. 2, reads: 'While preserving unity in essentials, let all members of the Church, according to the office entrusted to each, preserve a proper freedom in the various forms of spiritual life and discipline, in the variety of liturgical rites, and even in the theological elaborations of revealed truth.'

There is something here, particularly in respect of the phrases 'a hierarchy of truths', and 'freedom . . . even in the theological elaborations of revealed truth', which gives hope that such a line of approach as appeared to be emerging in the

6. *Works,* 1676 ed.

Commission's discussions may be an acceptable one to the Roman Catholic Church.

It is further supported by words in the allocution of Pope John at the opening of the Vatican Council: 'The substance of the ancient doctrine of the deposit of faith is one thing, and the way in which it is presented is another.' The reference by Pope Paul at the opening of the Third Session to 'pluralism in practice' points in a similar direction. (Both statements were discussed by the Bishop of Ripon and Professor Root in their paper on 'Unity and Comprehensiveness'[7]).

At a later stage, when a re-united Church is under discussion, the limits of comprehensiveness for both sides would naturally have to be examined, but as far as Stage I is concerned, this would not seem to be involved in the mutual recognition that each Church holds the essential faith.

The paper given to the Commission on the same subject ('To what extent can or should there be diversity in a united Church?') by Bishop J. G. Willebrands[8] was regarded by all as a most important opening up of this question and is very relevant to this question of the first Stage. Having indicated how history shows the existence of theological differences within the local Church, he asks if history can guide divided Christians today confronted with what Pope Paul called 'pluralism in essentials'. 'We have lived disunited for centuries. We have created doctrines and structures which have not remained within the communion of faith and charity but have broken it.' And again: '*The dialogue of charity . . .* will bring us to recognize and accept legitimate and authentically Christian differences which have developed during the centuries of separation.'

Is not this the whole point, and ought not the first Stage to be the simple recognition on the basis already referred to?

One may conclude with a quotation from the Roman Catholic theologian, Edward Schillebeeckx:

I personally believe that the Catholic Church must on the one hand allow ample space and liberty for theological pluralism (even for a certain pluralism in the interpretation of faith), but that on the other hand she must urge, more consistently than the

7. See above, pages 77–8.
8. See above, pages 60 ff., especially pages 72 and 73.

Lutheran Church in Germany has done, the fundamental credo of faith as the *canon fidei* or norm of faith, in spite of the uncertainty in all Christian Churches about the precise definitions of this fundamental confession of faith.[9]

B

Among the 'matters of practical difficulty, felt on either side' (Common Declaration of March 1966), there can be no doubt that, from the point of view of Anglicans and of all non-Roman Catholics, the question of mixed marriages is in the forefront. It is not too much to say that the present position is a major obstacle in the way of ecumenism, making it impossible for members of the Churches to deal with each other on that equal footing referred to in the Decree on Ecumenism (II. 9).

Since the Commission has recognized the urgency of this by requesting the setting up of a special body to deal with the question, there is no need to dwell further on details here.

Stage I would have little reality if, as well as mutual acknowledgment that both Churches hold the essential Christian faith, it were not possible for ordinary members of the Churches to have a candid relationship of charity and equality. At present, this relationship is greatly inhibited by the question of the mixed marriage provisions, and nothing would do more to remove suspicion and to create the beginnings of brotherhood than the removal of the obstacle at the inception of Stage I. It would be an undeniable assurance that Christians mean business as they approach the problem of disunity. From one aspect, it is a question of dealing with ecclesiastical legislation, but for many it is basically a matter of freedom (cf. Declaration on Religious Freedom, I. 5), while for all involved it is a human concern.

Discussions of the Commission also revealed that a second group of matters required attention, namely, the missionary situation, the sharing of church buildings where possible, as in new areas, the question of theological education, and the possibility of joint pronouncements. While each of these matters would require examination in depth, they would seem to fit in to the pattern of what might be the first Stage.

9. Quoted in an article in *The Irish Times* in Sept. 1967, by John Horgan.

A third group of questions of a liturgical nature appeared in the course of discussion, and clearly *the unifying effect of liturgy* ought to be taken full account of during Stage I. Steps could be taken to give effect to the Huntercombe proposals in respect of an agreed text for all common forms, e.g. Creeds, *Gloria in excelsis.* Since liturgical revision is now going on in most Churches of the Anglican Communion and in the Roman Catholic Church, this is the time to take practical steps to ensure linguistic uniformity.[10]

Yet another side of this, not touched on at the meeting, is the question of an agreed lectionary for use at the Eucharist. With the appearance of an Old Testament lection in the liturgical revisions of both Churches now in progress, a three-part common Eucharistic lectionary would be a possibility. Could Stage I involve a coming together of the various lectionary commissions and the pooling of their work with a view to a common usage? If such an arrangement could be made, it would greatly strengthen the effectiveness of Stage I at the level where it would most need strengthening.

Stage I would then involve dealing with the present canonical discipline in mixed marriages, the bringing in of common texts and forms, the making of joint pronouncements on matters of world concern, missionary competition, and theological education. This would 'bring the people on both sides along with us', to use a phrase used at our meeting and one which emphasized a vital aspect of Stage I.

This would be further helped by worship together and by the exchange of preachers. The *Directory on Ecumenism* of May 1967 might provide a basis for an agreed arrangement by both Churches suited to the nature of Stage I. The theological background would be similar to that of the Pope and Patriarch in that neither side should require from the other a positive acceptance of every article of the other's creed, e.g. the Patriarch specified the Vatican I definition of the Petrine primacy and infallibility. There are, of course, similarly differences as between Roman Catholics and Anglicans, and Anglicans would add Mariological definitions.

10. Since this paper was presented at the Malta meeting, such agreed English texts have been published by the International Consultation on English Texts: See *Prayers We Have In Common* (Geoffrey Chapman, London, 2nd ed. 1971)

The proposals for Stage I might then be summarized as follows:

I. Mutual recognition that each Church holds the essential Christian faith, neither being tied to a positive acceptance of all the beliefs held by the other.

II. The removal of the obstacle to ecumenism caused by mixed marriage legislation.

III. Joint examination of a. the missionary situation, b. sharing of buildings, c. theological education, d. the possibility of joint pronouncements.

IV. Joint action to ensure a. an agreed text for common forms, b. an agreed three-part lectionary for Eucharistic lessons from the Old Testament, the Epistle and the Gospels, and c. arrangements for common worship and for the interchange of preachers.

On this view, Stage I depends on mutual recognition of credal orthodoxy and on the removal of practical obstacles so that the members of both Churches may be able to regard each other 'not as rivals but as brothers and allies'.[11] This stage consists of the essential first movements if the hope expressed in the Common Declaration is to find fulfilment, that Anglicans and Roman Catholics shall treat one another with 'respect, esteem and fraternal love'.

Stage II

During the Commission's discussions, mention of the statement of the Pope and the Patriarch, and of the limited intercommunion between Roman Catholics and Orthodoxy as set out in the Vatican Council's Decree on Eastern Catholic Churches, gave rise to a suggestion as to the possibility of a similar relationship as between Roman Catholics and the Churches of the Anglican Communion.

The question, as framed by a Roman Catholic member of the Commission, was to the effect that, if the Petrine primacy, infallibility and Mariology, are the points dividing us from Anglicans, they also divide us form the Orthodox,[12] with whom

---

11. The Archbishop of Canterbury's booklet *Rome and Canterbury*, p. 2.
12. For the absence of Mariological definitions in Orthodoxy, see *The Orthodox Ethos* (1964), ed. A. J. Philippou, p. 147.

there is limited intercommunion, and so why not look for a similar relationship with Anglicans?

The section of the Decree which deals with 'Relations with the Brethren of Separated (Eastern) Churches' notes that 'a valid priesthood is preserved among Eastern clerics' and it lays down a new 'milder' and 'more lenient' policy in respect of *communicatio in sacris.*

An Orthodox Response to this, by Alexander Schmemann, while welcoming the Decree as a step forward, enters several reservations, particularly that the differences between East and West cannot be reduced to questions of rite and ethos in such a way as to isolate them from the doctrinal principles implied, for this constitutes 'the real issue between Roman Catholicism and Eastern Orthodoxy'. He also points out that the institution of Patriarchates ought not to be given 'an importance it does not have, in fact, in the Eastern Church' by regarding it in terms of 'a personal jurisdiction of the Patriarch over other bishops, which is alien to the Eastern canonical tradition, where the Patriarch or any other Primate is always a *primus inter pares'*. With regard to *communicatio in sacris*, he stresses that bilateral action is required which must express 'the consensus of all Orthodox Churches'.

If a parallel with the Roman/Anglican situation is to be drawn, there are several valuable pointers here, namely, the general theological context of such an agreement, the primacy, and the importance of bilateralism.

In this latter connection, the Bonn Agreement, which is one of full intercommunion, itemizes the details of a somewhat similar situation in three simple provisions:

(1) Each Communion recognizes the catholicity and independence of the other, and maintains its own.

(2) Each Communion agrees to admit members of the other communion to participate in the sacraments.

(3) Intercommunion does not require from either Communion the acceptance of all doctrinal opinion, sacramental devotion, or liturgical practice characteristic of the other, but implies that each believes the other to hold all the essentials of the Christian Faith.

Basically – apart from the fact that only limited intercommunion is visualized – this appears to be the situation as it actually is between the Roman Catholic and Orthodox Churches.

The Bonn Agreement, it will be recalled, followed the Old Catholic declaration in 1925 on Anglican Ordinations which was to the effect that the Old Catholic Church of Utrecht recognized 'the sufficiency of the rite of Edward VI as an adequate expression of the Catholic belief' and the intention of the Church of England 'to maintain the episcopal rule of the Church of antiquity' and had no reservations 'that the apostolic succession has not been broken in the Church of England'.[13]

Such an approach would involve, for Roman Catholics, the question of Anglican Orders. Anglicans have no corresponding difficulty as to the matter of fact, although they have had very real difficulty about notions of priesthood conceived in terms of 're-sacrificing'. Recent shifts of emphasis on this and allied questions since the Vatican Council make a difference here. For both sides there will surely be involved a radical looking again at concepts of the Church, the Ministry and the Sacraments, in the light of the New Testament's evidence and teaching, so that the question of Orders may be taken in relationship to what the Church is and to what its structures are.

To refer back to Bramhall's phrasing – if Stage I removes the obstacles to 'internal communion' then, logically, Stage II should confront the obstacles to 'external communion'.

If Stage II be taken as one of intercommunion, limited or not, what would be the steps by means of which practical proposals might come into view?

If, as appears to be indicated by the relationship of limited intercommunion between the Roman Catholic and Orthodox Churches, acceptance of the Petrine claims and Mariological dogmas is not essential for this limited intercommunion, from the Roman Catholic point of view, where should the approach to the Roman Catholic/Anglican situation commence?

As already suggested, the Ministry cannot be considered apart from the Church, so the approach to the problem would naturally be by way of questions such as: Who are the Church? What is the essential Ministry? What is the meaning of priest-

13. See G. K. A. Bell (ed.), *Documents on Christian Unity, Second Series* (1930), p. 64.

hood? This would include an examination of sacraments in relation to each of these questions.

This is, of course, somewhat simplified, but the first step in Stage II would be a joint examination of these questions in terms of the New Testament situation and the subsequent experience of the Church.

If a substantial measure of agreement were discovered in this area – and the work done by the writers of previous papers on the nature and extent of a legitimate diversity in the Church would fit in here – it would then be a natural second step to proceed to consider the specific question of Anglican Orders within this larger context, and to consider what practical moves would bring about intercommunion.

Two courses suggest themselves, and they ought not necessarily to be regarded as alternatives but rather as supplementing each other:

(1)   A joint re-examination of *Apostolicae Curae* in the light of a revised sacramental theology.

(2)   A joint examination of the position in the light of the Lambeth Appeal of 1920 and on the analogy of other Reunion schemes.

One could not, of course, at this stage forecast what attitude the Churches of the Anglican Communion would take to these two proposals, taken singly or together. It is a complex situation, with *Apostolicae Curae* on the one hand and, on the other, the complete absence of any doubt about their Orders on the part of Anglicans – as expressed, for instance, in the letter of July, 1925 in which the Archbishop of Canterbury accepts and receives the decision of the Old Catholic Church on Anglican Orders: 'For our own part we are sure, and have always been sure, that the apostolical succession has never been broken in the Church of England, and that a valid formula of consecration has been continually maintained.[14]

Respecting one another's consciences, Anglicans and Roman Catholics united in the dialogue of charity will also have to look at reasons and candidly examine together the theological and historical aspects. It may well be that some will favour thinking solely in terms of (2) (supra) but others may think that (2) implies (1).

14. Bell, *Documents on Christian Unity, A Selection 1920–30* (1955), p. 202.

In any event, the starting-point is the Church, and here Vatican II provides encouraging help in the shape of what may fairly be termed an ecclesiology with a changed emphasis. The shifting of the stress from a monarchical to a collegial concept of the Church, from a 'juridical' view to a view of the Church as an organism, comes closer to Anglican and Orthodox thinking. *Lumen Gentium* thinks in terms of the mystery of the Church, of the Church as the mystical Body, as a People, and apart from what Orthodox, Anglicans and Protestants would regard as the assumption of the basis of the Petrine claims, the document re-emphasizes the New Testament 'organic' idea of the Church. Professor Fairweather wrote in his paper at the Commission's first meeting: 'The constitution on the Church, as its teaching is assimilated by Roman Catholic theology, will inevitably bring the latter into close rapport with living Anglican, Protestant and Orthodox thought. Common study of the broad theme of *Lumen Gentium* should therefore be an advantageous starting-point for dialogue on the outstanding points of difference in the area of ecclesiology.' [15]

The first question then would be something like this: Within the framework of a consensus on ecclesiology – supposing that this could be achieved – could there be useful dialogue on the basis of an examination of the theological presuppositions of the Papal Constitution *Apostolicae Curae* in the light of what has been happening within the Roman Catholic Church since the second Vatican Council?

A recent article by Robert Adolfs, o.s.a. (in *New Christian*, 4 May 1967) suggests that there could be, with practical results, as his conclusion indicates: 'As a final suggestion, I would say that we should start working on a formula which would express the minimum requirements for a new form of corporate unity, which I would call "collegial communion" between the Anglican Church and the Roman Catholic Church.'

The article merits attention, not simply for the points it raises but also for the angle from which it raises them, namely that of post-Vatican II theology of the Church, the priesthood and the sacraments. This it contrasts with the theology of the Constitution which reflects, the author maintains, a type of

15. See above, page 53.

theological thinking superseded by the Vatican Council. It is on this changed emphasis that Adolfs bases his evaluation of the arguments of *Apostolicae Curae*, and his assessment of the 'special place' accorded by the Council's declaration to the Anglican Communion within the context of the restoration of unity.

Even more relevant because of its historical examination of the circumstances and its theological evaluation is an article, 'The Papal Condemnation of Anglican Orders: 1896', by John Jay Hughes in the *Journal of Ecumenical Studies*.[16] Quoting contemporary Roman Catholics who consider that the matter should be re-opened, the author writes: 'The growing conviction that Apostolicae Curae did not say the last word on Anglican Orders, and that the verdict of seventy years ago will have to be critically re-examined, has its roots in the one-sided procedure adopted in 1896.' He refers to the desire expressed at the time by some for a joint commission and clearly regards this as the procedure to be sought for now.

The second question – either taken in conjunction with the first or taken separately – would be in connection with the reconciliation of Ministries, what its content should be, and what its form and nature would be. The advisability and acceptability to both sides of this proposal would require careful examination, but we recall the agreement on the nature of the Apostolic Ministry as between *Lumen Gentium* and the Anglican statements read in connection with Anglican/Methodist conversations.

Stage II would then emerge either as one of limited intercommunion – and would thus be a penultimate phase – or it might become part of a final Stage which had as its objective full communion. These are the issues, and this might well be an approximation to the pattern of unity by stages, but at this point we cannot and should not attempt to impose a pattern.

———

Finally by way of general comment, some of the issues may be found merging into all the Stages, as discussion proceeds, rather than being confined to a particular Stage, with the result that the pattern of Stages reshapes itself. Accordingly,

16. Spring 1967, Vol. 4, No. 2, Temple University, Philadelphia.

the outline of Stages suggested in this paper is only a tentative one, and, in fact, could not presume to be anything else. But, since the request was to examine the possibilities of unity by stages, clearly some outlines were expected.

Yet no matter how the Stages involved are viewed in respect of form, content and timing (either in themselves, or in relation to each other, or to the ultimate objective), it also becomes clear that common investigation will be an important factor.

Such theological re-examination and enquiry, undertaken jointly, would have many topics to consider, all of which would bear in varying degrees on the question as to how the various Stages are to be viewed. For example, the whole subject of doctrinal development and the problems of meaning and interpretation seems to require review, and, as suggested already, there are the questions of the structures and channels of authority within the Church.

Doubtless there are many side-tracks on the approach to unity, such as premature proposals or too prolonged and diffuse theological debate, and others too. What the theologian may not forget is the desire of people for unity and their conviction, for whatever reasons, of the rightness of it. What the people should be helped to see by the theologian are the true dimensions of unity, no easy assignment. What both need to be helped to keep in the forefront is not only the how, but the why, for in this lies the true imperative and the primary motivation of the search for unity.

8

Unity: An Approach by Stages?

A PAPER PRESENTED AT MALTA,

DECEMBER/JANUARY 1967/8

BISHOP B. C. BUTLER, o.s.b.

(1) The Commission offers the following considerations in the light of the situation developing in Christianity as a whole, partly as a result of general world history and partly in consequence of the Ecumenical Movement in its present evolution. This situation can be summed up as follows: (a) the evolution of general world history makes Christian unity not only imperative but urgent. 'Without vision the people perishes'; and we believe that only Christianity can offer that vision, and that it is gravely impeded in its task by its present internal divisions. (b) Nearly all the major Christian communions and traditions are now engaged in a converging movement. (c) Not only ecclesiastical statesmen and/or theologians are involved in this movement but the masses of the faithful are feeling the desire for unity more and more keenly – and are sometimes impatient with the slowness of their leaders and thinkers. Together, these factors seem to create an unprecedented situation, calling – it may be thought – for unprecedented measures.

(2) But any such measures require, if not theological precedent, at least theological justification. This paper is concerned with possible measures in particular as regards the Roman Catholic and Anglican communions, and the question of theological justification for such measures.

(3) Such theological justification must commend itself alike to both our communions. And here we note certain already

existing theological agreements between us. The Pope and the Archbishop of Canterbury have already agreed that the basis of the Catholic/Anglican dialogue shall be 'Scripture and the Common Tradition'. In fact, we agree that the ultimate authority for all doctrine and theology is the Word Incarnate and the revelation entrusted to the Church of the apostolic age. And we agree that the revelation in Christ finds a normative record in the Bible (discussion would be needed with regard to the authority to be accorded to the deutero-canonical books or 'Apocrypha').

Scripture requires interpretation, and the Christian interpretation of the total biblical message takes shape in Tradition. Our two communions share a common past in Western mediaeval Christianity and in the 'undivided Church' of the early centuries; hence the relevance of the appeal to our 'Common Tradition'. This notion may need to be spelt out more fully. For instance, both our communions accept as authoritative the dogmatic formulations of the first four Ecumenical Councils (what about the Fifth, Sixth and Seventh Councils?). And both communions respect the teaching of the ancient Fathers (up to 1054) to the extent to which, in a developing tradition, this teaching approaches unanimity. More particularly, we are united in our acceptance of the three ancient Creeds as authoritative.

We refer here to the celebrated Lambeth Quadrilateral, which commends itself to us as 'valid' at least as far as it goes. It is possible that its terminology could be revised with advantage. We note the close convergence of the Anglican statement on the apostolic ministry (in reference to negotiations with the English Methodist Church) and Vatican II's teaching on the apostolic-episcopal college contained in *Lumen Gentium*.

Very difficult obstacles to organic unity between us remain, particularly in the field of doctrine (the papal primacy, infallibility, 'modern' Marian dogmas, for instance). On the other hand, it is common ground that 'the obedience of faith' by which man 'entrusts his whole self freely to God' is a personal assent to the revelation of God himself in Christ; and that the reality of this assent may co-exist with a defective apprehension of the material constituents of this revelation. And it could be argued that the doctrinal differences between our two communions relate less to 'the foundation of the Christian faith' than to elements in the deposit of faith which, while important, are less important than those elements on which we agree (cf. *De Revelatione* Nr. 5, *De Ecumenismo* Nr. 11).

(4) It is agreed between us that Christ's own will and desire for the unity of his disciples is a sufficient reason for seeking unity. It is also agreed that separated Christian bodies have severally preserved and fostered distinctive values which need to be preserved. And each of us would agree that authentically Christian doctrines and practices may have been better remembered and practised amongst others than amongst themselves.

(5) Reference has already been made to doctrinal divergences. At the heart of these are: (a) a differing theological evaluation of the divided state of Christianity. Anglicans would say that full visible unity is of the *bene esse* of the Church but not of its *esse*. The Roman Catholic Church teaches that it is of the *esse* of the Church and has therefore been preserved, in the visible communion of her own body, despite the tragic divisions of Christendom. (b) While both communions share a deep respect for the Common Tradition, the Roman Catholic Church holds that to the extent that this Tradition has been formulated in dogmatic definitions, or is expounded with moral unanimity by the episcopal college, it calls for not only respect but assent. We recognize the need of more reflection and discussion at this deep level of divergence between us.

(6) It appears to us that a relatively large area of common action and common prayer is already theologically justifiable by the measure of doctrinal agreement which we gladly acknowledge. We accept the theological notion of 'imperfect communion' set out in *De Ecumenismo*, and common action and prayer would appear to be desirable expressions of the amount of such 'communion' already existing between us. We would further emphasize that doctrinal agreement and practical joint action and prayer are likely to develop hand in hand and to exert a mutually beneficial influence; this means that experiments in co-operation can be envisaged, with a full recognition that not all of them will prove to have been useful.

(7) *De Ecumenismo* and the *Ecumenical Directory* have given a lead in practical matters to the Roman Catholic communion, and we think that few if any of the suggestions there made are unacceptable to the Anglican Communion. (We have ourselves, in previous statements, laid stress on some of these suggestions.)

(8) Such suggestions, taken together, would represent a 'first stage' in our common Approach to Unity. So far as we can see, while further suggestions might be forthcoming at this stage, there is no futher practical stage that can emerge short of 'intercommunion,' i.e. mutual authorization of what Roman Catholic theology calls 'communicatio in sacris', or participation in each other's liturgical prayer and sacraments.

(9) Intercommunion presents profound difficulties which require mature consideration. It is well known that these difficulties have dogged the path of the ecumenical movement. Particularly where mutual esteem has grown up on the basis of a common dedication to the cause of unity, separation from each other at the Lord's table has seemed almost intolerable. On the other hand, and apart from theological problems of a speculative kind, it must be acknowledged that intercommunion can itself be a hindrance to the cause of unity by appearing to remove the tension which gives it some of its dynamism. And in fact, some English Free Churchmen would agree that intercommunion between the membership of their Churches has not led to a desire, effective in practice, to overcome the remaining barriers to full communion.

(10) At the theological level, we agree with *De Ecumenismo* that '*communicatio in sacris* may not be regarded as a means to be used indiscriminately for the restoration of unity among Christians. Such worship depends chiefly on two principles. It should signify the unity of the Church, it should provide a sharing in the means of grace. The fact that it should signify unity generally rules out *communicatio in sacris*. Yet the gaining of a needed grace sometimes commends it.' (Nr. 8) It appears to us that, if other obstacles were overcome, it would rest with our respective Church authorities to determine in what conditions, if at all, intercommunion should be estab-

lished. Meanwhile, it may be apposite to point out that there was considerable intercommunion between East and West after 1054; that Vatican II envisaged a certain revival of this between the Orthodox and Roman Catholic communions today; and that Western Canon Law has long permitted the reception of sacraments from a validly ordained minister outside the communion of the Holy See *in extremis.*

(11) There is a particular obstacle between the Anglican and Roman Catholic communions with respect to possible intercommunion. The latter does not acknowledge the validity – though it does not contest the efficacy – of Anglican ordained ministry. This means that the Anglican Eucharist is not recognized as fully 'valid' by the Roman Catholic Church. We think that, for better mutual understanding, the notion of validity deserves fresh examination and elucidation. But for the overcoming of the obstacle, more than this would doubtless be necessary. At the theological level, it appears possible that a common deepening of our sacramental theology might be useful. At the more practical level, bearing in mind the analogous difficulties that have emerged in the quest of unity between the Anglican and other 'reformed' communions and the desire for some regularization of Protestant ministries to satisfy the Anglican difficulties in this matter, we venture to recall the affirmation of the Lambeth Conference of 1920 that the bishops there assembled would be prepared, in the interests of the achievement of full communion, to consider such 'regularization' of the Anglican ministry as might be required by the party with which unity was to be attained. While it is obvious that the Lambeth bishops of 1920 could not bind their successors, and that intercommunion is a much lesser goal than full communion, it appears to us that this declaration might well be borne in mind by both our communions if, on other grounds, intercommunion as a stage towards full communion should at some future date come to appear desirable.

(12) We commend to our respective Principals the possibility of joint statements by the major Christian leaders (e.g. the Pope, the Patriarch and the Archbishop) on world issues such as those covered by the recent papal encyclical *Populorum progressio.* A dominant reason for the quest of Christian unity

is that our divisions make our witness to the world less effective. Such common pronouncements, which do not require full communion or even intercommunion as a pre-condition, would go some way to unify our witness.

(13) We wish to emphasize that, in our view, there is no automatic implication in Stage I of subsequently accepting Stage II; still less, that Stage II will inevitably lead on to Stage III, i.e. full communion. Unity, to the extent to which it comes about, will be the work of the Holy Spirit, and we cannot dictate dates or goals to him. We have thought it to be our more modest task, to outline a possible road towards further unity, and to examine or to indicate the theological issues involved.

9

The Malta Report

REPORT OF THE ANGLICAN/ROMAN CATHOLIC
JOINT PREPARATORY COMMISSION
AFTER MEETING AT GAZZADA
(*9 to 13 January 1967*),
HUNTERCOMBE MANOR
(*31 August to 4 September 1967*),
AND MALTA
(*30 December 1967 to 3 January 1968*)

I

1. The visit of the Archbishop of Canterbury to Pope Paul VI in March 1966, and their decision to constitute an Anglican/ Roman Catholic Joint Preparatory Commission, marked a new stage in relations between our two Churches. The three meetings of the Commission, held during 1967 at Gazzada, Huntercombe, and in Malta, were characterized not only by a spirit of charity and frankness, but also by a growing sense of urgency, penitence, thankfulness, and purpose: of urgency, in response to the pressure of God's will, apprehended as well in the processes of history and the aspirations and achievements of men in his world as in the life, worship, witness, and service of his Church; of penitence, in the conviction of our shared responsibility for cherishing animosities and prejudices which for four hundred years have kept us apart, and prevented our attempting to understand or resolve our differences; of thankfulness for the measure of unity which through baptism into Christ we already share, and for our recent growth towards greater unity and mutual understanding; of purpose, in our determination that the work begun in us by God shall

be brought by his grace, to fulfilment in the restoration of his peace to his Church and his world.

2. The members of the Commission have completed the preparatory work committed to them by compiling this report which they submit for their consideration to His Holiness the Pope and His Grace the Archbishop. The Decree on Ecumenism recognizes that among the Western Communions separated from the Roman See the Churches of the Anglican Communion 'hold a special place'. We hope in humility that our work may so help to further reconciliation between Anglicans and Roman Catholics as also to promote the wider unity of all Christians in their common Lord. We share the hope and prayer expressed in the common declaration issued by the Pope and the Archbishop after their meeting that 'a serious dialogue founded on the Gospels and on the ancient common traditions may lead to that unity in truth for which Christ prayed'.

3. We record with great thankfulness our common faith in God our Father, in our Lord Jesus Christ, and in the Holy Spirit; our common baptism in the one Church of God; our sharing of the holy Scriptures, of the Apostles' and Nicene Creeds, the Chalcedonian definition, and the teaching of the Fathers; our common Christian inheritance for many centuries with its living traditions of liturgy, theology, spirituality, Church order, and mission.

4. Divergences since the sixteenth century have arisen not so much from the substance of this inheritance as from our separate ways of receiving it. They derive from our experience of its value and power, from our interpretation of its meaning and authority, from our formulation of its content, from our theological elaboration of what it implies, and from our understanding of the manner in which the Church should keep and teach the Faith. Further study is needed to distinguish between those differences which are merely apparent, and those which are real and require serious examination.

5. We agree that revealed Truth is given in holy Scripture and formulated in dogmatic definitions through thought-forms and language which are historically conditioned. We are

encouraged by the growing agreement of theologians in our two Communions on methods of interpreting this historical transmission of revelation. We should examine further and together both the way in which we assent to and apprehend dogmatic truths and the legitimate means of understanding and interpreting them theologically. Although we agree that doctrinal comprehensiveness must have its limits, we believe that diversity has an intrinsic value when used creatively rather than destructively.

6. In considering these questions within the context of the present situation of our two Communions, we propose particularly as matter for dialogue the following possible convergences of lines of thought: first, between the traditional Anglican distinction of internal and external communion and the distinction drawn by the Vatican Council between full and partial communion; secondly, between the Anglican distinction of fundamentals from non-fundamentals and the distinction implied by the Vatican Council's references to a 'hierarchy of truths' (Decree on Ecumenism, 11), to the difference between 'revealed truths' and 'the manner in which they are formulated' (Pastoral Constitution on the Church in the Modern World, 62), and to diversities in theological tradition being often 'complementary rather than conflicting' (Decree on Ecumenism, 17).

II

7. We recommend that the second stage in our growing together begin with an official and explicit affirmation of mutual recognition from the highest authorities of each Communion. It would acknowledge that both Communions are at one in the faith that the Church is founded upon the revelation of God the Father, made known to us in the Person and work of Jesus Christ, who is present through the Holy Spirit in the Scriptures and his Church, and is the only Mediator between God and Man, the ultimate Authority for all our doctrine. Each accepts the basic truths set forth in the ecumenical Creeds and the common tradition of the ancient Church, although neither Communion is tied to a positive acceptance of all the beliefs and devotional practices of the other.

8. In every region where each Communion has a hierarchy, we propose an annual joint meeting of either the whole or some considerable representation of the two hierarchies.

9. In the same circumstances we further recommend:

(a) Constant consultation between committees concerned with pastoral and evangelistic problems including, where appropriate, the appointment of joint committees.

(b) Agreements for joint use of churches and other ecclesiastical buildings, both existing and to be built, wherever such use is helpful for one or other of the two Communions.

(c) Agreements to share facilities for theological education, with the hope that all future priests of each Communion should have attended some course taught by a professor of the other Communion. Arrangements should also be made where possible for temporary exchange of students.

(d) Collaboration in projects and institutions of theological scholarship to be warmly encouraged.

10. Prayer in common has been recommended by the Decree on Ecumenism and provisions for this common worship are to be found in the *Directory* (para. 56). We urge that they be implemented.

11. Our similar liturgical and spiritual traditions make extensive sharing possible and desirable; for example, in non-eucharistic services, the exploration of new forms of worship, and retreats in common. Religious orders of similar inspiration in the two Communions are urged to develop a special relationship.

12. Our closeness in the field of sacramental belief leads us further to recommend that on occasion the exchange of preachers for the homily during the celebration of the Eucharist be also permitted, without prejudice to the more general regulations contained in the *Directory*.

13. Since our liturgies are closely related by reason of their common source, the ferment of liturgical renewal and reform now engaging both our Communions provides an unprecedented opportunity for collaboration. We should co-operate, and not take unilateral action, in any significant changes in the seasons and major holy days of the Christian Year; and we

should experiment together in the devolopment of a common eucharistic lectionary. A matter of special urgency in view of the advanced stage of liturgical revision in both Communions is that we reach agreement on the vernacular forms of those prayers, hymns, and responses which our people share in common in their respective liturgies. (A list of these texts is appended.) We recommend that this be taken up without delay.

We are gratified that collaboration in this work has been initiated by the exchange of observers and consultants in many of our respective liturgical commissions. Especially in matters concerning the vernacular, we recommend that representatives of our two Communions (not excluding other Christian bodies with similar liturgical concerns) be associated on a basis of equality both in international and in national and regional committees assigned this responsibility.

14. We believe that joint or parallel statements from our Church leaders at international, national, and local level on urgent human issues can provide a valuable form of Christian witness.

15. In the field of missionary strategy and activity ecumenical understanding is both uniquely valuable and particularly difficult. Very little has hitherto been attempted in this field between our two Communions and, while our other recommendations of course apply to the young Churches and mission areas, we propose further the institution at international level of an official joint consultation to consider the difficulties involved and the co-operation which should be undertaken.

16. The increasing number of mixed marriages points to the need for a thorough investigation of the doctrine of marriage in its sacramental dimension, its ethical demands, its canonical status, and its pastoral implications. It is hoped that the work of the Joint Commission on Marriage will be promptly initiated and vigorously pursued, and that its recommendations will help to alleviate some of the difficulties caused by mixed marriages, to indicate acceptable changes in Church regulations, and to provide safeguards against the dangers which threaten to undermine family life in our time.

III

17. We cannot envisage in detail what may be the issues and demands of the final stage in our quest for the full, organic unity of our two Communions. We know only that we must be constant in prayer for the grace of the Holy Spirit in order that we may be open to his guidance and judgement, and receptive to each other's faith and understanding. There remain fundamental theological and moral questions between us where we need immediately to seek together for reconciling answers. In this search we cannot escape the witness of our history; but we cannot resolve our differences by mere reconsideration of, and judgement upon, the past. We must press on in confident faith that new light will be given us to lead us to our goal.

18. The fulfilment of our aim is far from imminent. In these circumstances the question of accepting some measure of sacramental intercommunion apart from full visible unity is being raised on every side. In the minds of many Christians no issue is today more urgent. We cannot ignore this, but equally we cannot sanction changes touching the very heart of Church life, eucharistic communion, without being certain that such changes would be truly Christian. Such certainty cannot be reached without more and careful study of the theology implied.

19. We are agreed that among the conditions required for intercommunion are both a true sharing in faith and the mutual recognition of ministry. The latter presents a particular difficulty in regard to Anglican Orders according to the traditional judgement of the Roman Church. We believe that the present growing together of our two Communions and the needs of the future require of us a very serious consideration of this question in the light of modern theology. The theology of the ministry forms part of the theology of the Church and must be considered as such. It is only when sufficient agreement has been reached as to the nature of the priesthood and the meaning to be attached in this context to the word 'validity' that we could proceed, working always jointly, to the application of this doctrine to the Anglican ministry of today. We

would wish to re-examine historical events and past documents only to the extent that they can throw light upon the facts of the present situation.

20. In addition, a serious theological examination should be jointly undertaken on the nature of authority with particular reference to its bearing on the interpretation of the historic faith to which both our Communions are committed. Real or apparent differences between us come to the surface in such matters as the unity and indefectibility of the Church and its teaching authority, the Petrine primacy, infallibility, and Mariological definitions.

21. In continuation of the work done by our Commission, we recommend that it be replaced by a Permanent Joint Commission responsible (in co-operation with the Secretariat for Promoting Christian Unity and the Church of England Council on Foreign Relations in association with the Anglican Executive Officer) for the oversight of Roman Catholic/Anglican relations, and the co-ordination of future work undertaken together by our two Communions.

22. We also recommend the constitution of two joint sub-commissions, responsible to the Permanent Commission, to undertake two urgent and important tasks:

ONE to examine the question of intercommunion, and the related matters of Church and Ministry;
THE OTHER to examine the question of authority, its nature, exercise, and implications.

We consider it important that adequate money, secretarial assistance, and research facilities should be given to the Commission and its sub-commissions in order that their members may do their work with thoroughness and efficiency.

23. We also recommend joint study of moral theology to determine similarities and differences in our teaching and practice in this field.

24. In concluding our Report we cannot do better than quote

the words of those by whom we were commissioned, and to whom, with respect, we now submit it:

In willing obedience to the command of Christ Who bade His disciples love one another, they declare that, with His help, they wish to leave in the hands of the God of mercy all that in the past has been opposed to this precept of charity, and that they make their own the mind of the Apostle which he expressed in these words: 'Forgetting those things which are behind, and reaching forth unto those things which are before, I press towards the mark for the prize of the high calling of God in Christ Jesus' (Phil. 3.13–14).

> The Common Declaration by Pope Paul VI
> and the Archbishop of Canterbury
> 24 March 1966

Malta, 2 January 1968

Appendix

SOME COMMON LITURGICAL FORMS [1]

A. The Lord's Prayer
   The Apostles' and Nicene Creeds
   The Salutation, Responses
   The Gloria Patri
   The Kyrie
   The Gloria in excelsis
   The Sursum corda, Sanctus, and Benedictus qui venit
   The Agnus Dei

B. The Te Deum
   The Canticles: Benedictus, Magnificat, and Nunc Dimittis

C. The Psalter

---

1. Except for the Psalter, agreed texts of almost all of these will now be found in *Prayers We Have In Common* referred to on p. 93, note 10.

Anglican/Roman Catholic Joint Preparatory Commission

LIST OF MEMBERS[2]

Roman Catholic Church

The Most Rev. Charles Helmsing, Bishop of Kansas City–St Joseph (JOINT CHAIRMAN)
The Most Rev. J. G. M. Willebrands, titular Bishop of Mauriana
The Most Rev. William Z. Gomes, Bishop of Poona
The Right Rev. Langton D. Fox, titular Bishop of Maura
The Right Rev. Christopher Butler, o.s.b., titular Bishop of Nova Barbara
The Rev. Louis Bouyer
The Rev. Father George Tavard, A.A.
The Rev. Michael Richards
The Rev. Father John Keating, c.s.p.
The Rev. Adrian Hastings
The Rev. Camillus Hay, o.f.m.
The Very Rev. Canon W. A. Purdy

Anglican Communion

The Right Rev. J. R. H. Moorman, Bishop of Ripon (JOINT CHAIRMAN)
[3] The Right Rev. W. G. H. Simon, Bishop of Llandaff
The Right Rev. C. H. W. de Soysa, Bishop of Colombo
The Right Rev. E. G. Knapp-Fisher, Bishop of Pretoria
The Right Rev. H. R. McAdoo, Bishop of Ossory, Ferns, and Leighlin
The Rev. Canon James Atkinson
The Rev. Canon Eric Kemp
The Rev. Professor Howard E. Root
The Rev. Dr. Massey H. Shepherd Jr.
The Rev. Professor Eugene R. Fairweather
The Rev. Professor Albert T. Mollegen
The Rev. Canon John Findlow
The Rev. Canon John R. Satterthwaite

2. As given in the Malta Report, of which this is part. A few differences in final membership will be noticed, compared with the original list on pages 8–9, above, as the Introduction, pp. 10, 14 and 15, explains.
3. Unfortunately unable to attend the third meeting.

10

Letter from His Eminence Cardinal Augustin Bea to His Grace the Archbishop of Canterbury

10 June 1968

Secretariat for
Promoting
Christian Unity

Vatican City,
10 June 1968

Your Grace,

It is with heartfelt joy that I am sending to you the personal letter of the Holy Father in which he expresses his satisfaction and gratitude for the work of the Anglican/Roman Catholic Joint Preparatory Commission, which after its sessions held during 1967 at Gazzada, Huntercombe, and in Malta, has completed the preparatory work committed to its members by compiling at its last session a report which makes concrete proposals for the continuation of the work done by the Commission. Despite our diversities we have some truths in common, which are very important and oblige us to travel the road towards unity.

His Holiness has charged me to explain more in detail, how this continuation, on the basis of the work already done, should further be planned:

We approve the idea and agree that further studies be made on the points related in the report:

(a) on a common declaration of faith between Catholics and Anglicans;

(b) on liturgical problems of common concern for the Roman Catholic Church and the Anglican Communion;

(c) on the possibility of co-ordinate action through joint or parallel statements on urgent human issues at international, national, and local level;

(d) on the problems and difficulties which arise in the field of missionary strategy and activity of the Church, and the possibility of co-operation;

(e) on the theological and pastoral problems of the doctrine of marriage and the difficulties caused by mixed marriages;

(f) on the ecclesiological principles of the Roman Catholic Church and the Anglican Communion in connection with the problem of sacramental intercommunion;

(g) on the theology of the Church and the theology of the ministry in connection with the nature of the priesthood and the application of this doctrine to the Anglican ministry of today;

(h) on the nature of authority in the Church and its concrete form in the teaching authority, in the Petrine primacy, etc.;

(i) on problems of moral theology;

(j) on the application of practical directions given in the Decree of the Second Vatican Council on Ecumenism and in the Directory issued by our Secretariat for Promoting Christian Unity.

Moreover we approve certain practical recommendations made in the report such as:

(a) periodical joint meetings in regions where both the Roman Catholic Church and the Anglican Communion have a hierarchy of either the whole or some considerable representation of the two hierarchies;

(b) consultations on pastoral problems of evangelization in the modern world;

(c) common prayers, according to the rules of the Directory issued by our Secretariat for Promoting Christian Unity;

(d) development under the direction of the respective Superiors of a special relationship between religious orders of similar inspiration in the two communions.

Other practical recommendations, however, such as agreements for joint use of churches, and agreements to share facilities for theological education and temporary exchange of students require further investigation and especially consultation with the appropriate authorities (the episcopal conferences and the competent authority in Rome).

In order to assure the continuation of the work done by the Anglican/Roman Catholic Joint Preparatory Commission and to carry out the proposals for further studies and activities, we accept the recommendations made by the Commission:

(a) that the Commission be replaced by a Joint Commission responsible for the oversight of Roman Catholic/Anglican relations, and the co-ordination of future work undertaken together by the Roman Catholic Church and the Anglican Communion;

(b) the constitution of joint sub-commissions, responsible to the Joint Commission, which are necessary for the execution of the programme if approved by the authorities on both sides;

(c) the Secretariat for Promoting Christian Unity and the Church of England Council on Foreign Relations in association with the Anglican Executive Officer should study the methods and concrete ways in which the practical recommendations, as far as they have been approved on both sides, can be realized.

Concerning the question of the publication of the Malta Report, we believe it is better not to give the report for publication to the press. In some of its phrases, the formulation seems not quite clear and exact. Its publication through the press might create the impression that the report represents more than a report of a preparatory commission and even create among the Bishops of the Church the impression that the Report has been already approved by the competent authorities in all its details and that it was communicated to them for implementation. But in fact we are still at a phase of study and for the present moment we prefer that further steps be taken after careful study and with approval of the official authorities on both sides. Of course we do not intend to prevent Your Grace from communicating the content of the report to the members of the Lambeth Conference, if you would think this advisable in order to have their reactions and their proposals for the continuation of the dialogue and the co-operation.

I express my sincere hope that with the support of the prayers of all the faithful through the grace of God the Churches may be led by him who is the way, the truth, and the life, to the unity in the Holy Spirit, 'That there may be one visible Church of God, a Church truly universal and sent forth to the whole world that the world may be converted to the Gospel and so be saved, to the glory of God' (Decree on Ecumenism, 1).

With a warm and heartfelt greeting in the name of our common Lord and with a renewal of my personal pledge of prayers for the guidance of the Holy Spirit in your momentous labours this summer.

I remain,

Yours devotedly in Christ,

(signed) ✠ AUG. CARD. BEA,
✠ J. G. M. WILLEBRANDS
Secr.

II

Resolutions and Report of the Lambeth Conference 1968 on Anglican/Roman Catholic Relations

A. RESOLUTIONS

52. The Conference welcomes the proposals made in the report of Section III which concern Anglican relations with the Roman Catholic Church.

53. The Conference recommends the setting up of a Permanent Joint Commission, for which the Anglican delegation should be chosen by the Lambeth Consultative Body (or its successor) and be representative of the Anglican Communion as a whole.

54. In view of the urgent pastoral questions raised by mixed marriages the Conference welcomes the work of the Joint Commission on the Theology of Marriage and its Application to Mixed Marriages, and urges its speedy continuance.

B. REPORT OF SECTION III:

The Renewal of the Church in Unity

RELATIONS WITH THE ROMAN CATHOLIC CHURCH

In the 'Common Declaration', signed in Rome on 24 March 1966, the Pope and the Archbishop of Canterbury gave thanks to Almighty God for the new atmosphere of Christian fellowship now existing between the two Churches, and declared their intention of inaugurating 'a serious dialogue which, founded on the Gospels and on the ancient common traditions, may lead to that unity in truth, for which Christ prayed'. This dialogue, they declared, was to include 'not only theological matters such as Scripture, Tradition and Liturgy, but also matters of practical difficulty felt on either side'.

It was as a result of this Declaration that a Joint Preparatory Commission was set up; and the Section received with gratitude the report issued as a result of the three meetings of that Commission.

Essential to such meetings is the spirit in which they are undertaken. For our part we recognize in penitence that many of our past attitudes and actions have contributed to our unhappy divisions and that there are still many things in us for which we must ask the forgiveness of God and of our fellow Christians. Yet we are thankful for the many signs of renewal of the spirit of unity in ourselves and in others.

Together with the Roman Catholic Church we confess our faith in God, Father, Son, and Holy Spirit, as witnessed by the holy Scriptures, the Apostles' and Nicene Creeds, and by the teaching of the Fathers of the early Church. We have one baptism and recognize many common features in our heritage. At the same time substantial divergences exist, many of which have arisen since the sixteenth century, in such matters as the unity and indefectibility of the Church and its teaching authority, the Petrine primacy, infallibility, and Mariological definitions, as well as in some moral problems. These matters will require serious study so that they may be carefully identified and, under the guidance of the Spirit, resolved. This task must be undertaken in the light of the challenge to the whole Church of God presented by the modern world, and in the context of the mission of the Church throughout the world and to all sorts and conditions of men.

SIGNS OF PROGRESS

Relations between Anglicans and Roman Catholics are progressing in various ways and to varying degrees in many places. Examples include common services of prayer and thanksgiving, the joint use of churches, the exchange of preachers, co-operation in theological education, and meetings of official commissions and informal groups. With due regard to individual consciences, we endorse and encourage these developments where local circumstances permit the avoidance of misunderstanding.

We rejoice that the new attitude towards Scripture, expressed in the Constitution on Divine Revelation, has led to co-operation in biblical studies and in the work of the United Bible Societies.

Liturgical renewal and reform represent a field where co-operation is urgent. Unilateral action in regard to the liturgical year and the vernacular forms used by our people is to be avoided.

The Christian witness being given by our clergy and laity in many urgent human issues, in many cases in close association with Roman Catholics, claims our support and our prayers. Where such witness may be strengthened by joint or parallel statements by church leaders these should be issued.

We welcome the increasing signs of mutual recognition, not least in practical acts on both sides, of the reality of Anglican and Roman Catholic ministry in the whole Body of Christ on earth.

A PERMANENT JOINT COMMISSION

We recommend the setting up of a Permanent Joint Commission, our delegation to be chosen by the Lambeth Consultative Body or its successor and to be representative of the Anglican Communion as a whole. This commission or its sub-commissions should consider the question of intercommunion in the context of a true sharing in faith and the mutual recognition of ministry, and should also consider in the light of the new biblical scholarship the orders of both Churches and the theology of ministry which forms part of the theology of the Church and can only be considered as such. The hope for the future lies in a fresh and broader approach to the understanding of apostolic succession and of the priestly office. On this line we look for a new joint appraisal of church orders.

Conversations between Anglicans and Roman Catholics should be conducted with due regard to the multiplicity of conversations also in progress with other Churches. In them all we propose to hold fast the principles of Catholic truth as we have been given to understand them, though we realize that, in renewed obedience to the Holy Spirit, we must at all times be willing to go forward adventurously.

INDEX

Absolution, 56, 77
Acts of the Apostles, 62, 63, 69, 70
Adolfs, Fr. Robert, 98, 99
Africa, 7
Agnus Dei, 114
Alexandria, 67, 68
Allmen, J.-J. von, 63
Ambrose, St., 66
America, 7
Amsterdam, 28
Ananias, 63
Ancel, Bishop of Lyons, 31
Andrewes, Lancelot, 85
Anglican Communion, 1, 3, 7, 25, 31, 36, 37, 39, 48, 49, 76, 97, 120, 122
— Executive Officer, 7, 118
— formularies, 40, 90
—/Methodist Conversations, 21, 99, 102
— Orders, validity of, 22, 23, 43, 58, 59, 96, 97, 99, 105, 112, 117, 122
Anicetus, 65
Antioch, 67, 68
Apocalypse, 61
Apocrypha, 102
Apostles, Twelve, 19, 62, 63
Apostles' Creed, 4, 7, 89, 108, 114, 121
Apostolicae Curae, 27, 43, 97, 98, 99
Apostolic Succession, 17, 90, 96, 97, 122
Arianism, 66, 80
Asia, 7

Asia Minor, 64, 68
Assumption of the Blessed Virgin Mary, 16, 43, 57, 83
Athanasian Creed, 89
Athanasius, St., 66
Athenagoras I, Ecumenical Patriarch, 73, 87, 93, 94, 105
Atkinson, Canon James, 8, 12, 15, 115
Atonement, 81
Augustine of Canterbury, St., 1, 3, 66
— of Hippo, St., 65, 66
Australia, 15
Authority, 11, 12, 15, 17, 18, 20, 21, 42, 45, 46, 52, 53, 60, 63, 64, 74, 81, 82, 85, 88, 89, 100, 102, 109, 113, 117, 121

Bagatti, Fr., 68
Baptism, 58, 65, 86, 107, 108, 121
Barrow, Isaac, 42
Basil, St., 66
Bea, Cardinal Augustin, 25, 29, 116ff.
Bede, the Venerable, 66
Bell, Bishop G. K. A., 96, 97
Bellarmine, Cardinal, 85
Benedictus, 114
Benedictus qui venit, 114
Bettenson, H., 87
Bible, *see* Scripture(s)
Biblical Institute, 29
Biblical renewal, 10, 28–30
Birth control, 83
Bishops, *see* Episcopacy

Bonn Agreement, 20, 87, 88, 90, 95, 96
Book of Common Prayer, 47
Bouyer, Fr. Louis, 9, 12, 18, 19, 21, 115
Bradshaw Society, 30
Bramhall, John, 89, 90, 96
Branch Theory, 27
Butler, Bishop B. C., 15, 18, 20, 21, 22, 23, 101ff., 115
Byzantium, *see* Constantinople

Calvinists, 48
Cambridge, 42
Camden Society, 30
Camelot, P. Th., 67, 68
Canadian Roman Catholic Commission on Ecumenism, 9
Canon Law, 28, 105
Canterbury, 74, 76
—, Archbishop of, Dr. Randall Davidson, 97
—, — —, Dr. Michael Ramsey, 1ff., 5, 6, 7, 13, 21, 24, 25, 26, 36, 76, 84, 94, 102, 105, 107, 108, 114, 116, 118, 120; Commission on Roman Catholic Relations of, 8; Common Declaration of with Pope Paul VI, 1ff., 6, 26, 84, 87, 92, 94, 102, 108, 114, 120; Representative at Vatican of, 8; Visit to Rome of (1966), 1ff., 5, 6, 36
—, — —, Dr. William Temple, 32
—, St. Augustine of, 1, 3, 66
Cardwell, E., 43
Casulanus, 66
Cazelles, Prof. H., 69
Celibacy of the Clergy, 65, 83
Chalcedon, Council of, 67, 68, 81, 108
Christian Unity, Association for Promoting, 26
Christian Year, 110, 122

Christology, 66, 67
Church, authority of and in, 11, 15, 17, 46, 52, 56, 100, 113, 117, 121; doctrine of, 11, 12, 15, 16, 17, 18, 19, 20, 23, 32, 33, 34, 38, 39, 51, 53, 65, 71, 72, 96, 98, 103, 112, 113, 117, 121, 122; structure of, 12, 17, 24, 51, 53, 62, 70, 96, 100; teaching office of, 11, 24, 46, 51, 52, 85, 113, 117; undivided, 17; uniqueness of, 11, 18
— buildings, joint use of, 13, 22, 92, 94, 110, 118, 121
— and State, 11
Church Times, 25
Clergy, 13, 17, 18, 22, 110
Collegiality, *see* Episcopal College
Colossians, Epistle to the, 61
Comprehensiveness, 11, 21, 40, 66, 74–83 *passim,* 91, 109
Consensus fidelium, 46
Constantinople (Byzantium), 65, 66, 73
Constantinopolitan Creed, 60, 67
Corinth, Church of, 63
Cornelius, 63
Council(s), 4, 17, 40, 41, 43, 45, 46, 47, 65, 68, 85, 89, 102
Council on Foreign Relations, Church of England, 8, 113, 118
Counter-Reformation, 15, 42, 52
Creed(s), 40, 41, 47, 60, 77, 85, 88, 89, 90, 92, 93, 102, 108, 109, 114, 121
Cross, Dr. F. L., 88
Cyril of Alexandria, St., 67, 73

David, King, 70
Davidson, Archbishop Randall, *see* Canterbury
Davis, Fr. Charles, 9, 10

Dean, Bishop Ralph, 7
Denzinger, H., 67
Devotion, 21, 24, 56, 57, 82, 83,
    95, 109
Diekman, G., 31
Diversity, 12, 20, 21, 60–73
    passim, 74ff., 91, 97, 103,
    109
Doctrine, authority of and in,
    11, 45ff., 51, 52, 102, 109;
    Development in, 81, 100
Dogma(s), 21, 22, 40, 41, 42, 52,
    57, 96, 103, 108, 109
Downside Abbey, 15
Duns Scotus, 80

Easter, 64, 65
Economy, 67
Ecumenical Movement, 27, 28,
    38, 76, 101
Ecumenism, Directory on,
    (1967), 22, 78, 93, 104, 110,
    117
—, Instruction on, (1949), 28
Education, 11, 13
Edward VI, King, 96
Egypt, 68
Encyclicals, Papal: *Ad omnes
    Episcopos Angliae* (1864),
    26, 27; *Divino Afflante
    Spiritu* (1943), 29, 30;
    Mediator Dei (1947), 31;
    Mortalium Animos (1928),
    26, 27; *Populorum
    Progressio* (1967), 105;
    Providentissimus Deus
    (1893), 29, 30
Ephesians, Epistle to the, 61,
    69
Ephesus, Council of, 67
Episcopacy (Bishops), 11, 13, 17,
    18, 22, 72, 77, 89, 96
Episcopal College
    (Collegiality), 18, 20, 33, 53,
    54, 72, 81, 98, 102, 103
Epistles, 94
Ethiopian Eunuch, 63

Eucharist, 11, 14, 42, 44, 48, 49,
    54, 58, 59, 62, 86, 93, 105,
    110
Eucharistic sacrifice, 42, 48, 49,
    58
Europe, 7
Eusebius, 64, 65
Evangelicals, representative of,
    14
Evangelistic problems, 110

Fairweather, Prof. E. R., 8, 10,
    11, 12, 16, 37ff., 98, 115
Faith, 17, 39, 68, 70, 78, 81, 84,
    85, 86, 87, 88, 89, 92, 94,
    102, 103, 108, 109, 113, 116
Faith and Order, 27, 52
Fasting, 64, 65
Fathers of the Church, 40, 41,
    45, 79, 85, 88, 89, 102, 108,
    121
Findlow, Canon J., 7, 8, 22, 23,
    115
Fox, Bishop Langton D., 9, 12,
    18, 115
Free Churches, 104
Freedom (Liberty), 12, 20, 60,
    62, 63, 64, 66, 74, 90, 92

Galatians, Epistle to the, 70
    86
Galilee, 68
Gallier, P., 67
Gamaliel, Rabbi, 70
Gaul, 64
Gazzada, 7, 10ff., 22, 23, 24, 26,
    37, 74, 82, 107, 116
Gentile-Christian Church, 68–9
Germany, 92
Gloria in Excelsis, 93, 114
Gloria Patri, 114
Gomes, Bishop William, 9, 24,
    115
Gospel(s), 2, 3, 11, 33, 35, 38, 39,
    41, 42, 45, 46, 47ff., 58, 63,
    69, 72, 74, 78, 84, 94, 108,
    119, 120

Grace, 41, 48, 49, 50, 54, 55, 56, 57, 58, 70, 86, 104
Great Britain, 7
Gregory the Great, Pope, 66

Hamer, Fr. Jerome, 7
Hammond, Henry, 88
Hastings, Fr. Adrian, 9, 12, 16, 17, 20, 115
Hay, Fr. Camillus, 15, 18, 115
Helmsing, Bishop Charles, 9, 10, 19, 20, 115
Henderson, Prof. Ian, 74
Herder Correspondence, 25
Hierarchy, 53, 110
Hierarchy of Truths, 20, 79, 90, 109
High Church, 76, 77
Hilary, St., 66, 80
Holy Spirit, 1, 2, 3, 4, 14, 16, 17, 22, 24, 36, 38, 61, 62, 63, 64, 66, 67, 73, 77, 82, 106, 108, 109, 112, 119, 121, 122
Horgan, John, 92
Hughes, Fr. J. J., 99
Huntercombe, 14ff., 23, 24, 60, 74, 84, 87, 93, 107, 116

Immaculate Conception of the Blessed Virgin Mary, 43, 57
Indefectibility, 113, 121
Indian Roman Catholic Commission on Ecumenism, 9
Indulgences, 56
Infallibility, 17, 19, 22, 43, 44, 46, 54, 85, 88, 93, 94, 102, 113, 121
Innocent I, Pope, 66
Intercommunion, 21, 22, 94, 95, 96, 97, 99, 104, 105, 106, 109, 112, 113, 117, 122
International Consultation on English Texts, 93
Invocation of Saints, 42
Ireland, Church of, 14
Irish Times, 92

Irenaeus of Lyons, St., 64, 65
Israel, People of, 60, 61

James, St., 69, 70
Januarius, 66
Jerusalem, 70
—, Council of, 65, 68, 69
Jesus Christ, 1, 2, 3, 4, 6, 16, 18, 24, 32, 33, 34, 36, 45, 49, 53, 56, 58, 60, 61, 62, 63, 64, 65, 67, 70, 73, 77, 84, 86, 102, 103, 107, 108, 109, 114, 119, 120, 121
John of Antioch, 67, 73
— XXIII, Pope, 77, 91
—, St., 62
Journal of Ecumenical Studies, 99
Judaea, 68
Judaeo-Christian Church, 68–70
Judaism, 68, 70
Jurisdiction, 19, 95
Justification, 42, 49, 50, 55

Keating, Fr. John, 9, 12, 17, 115
Kemp, Canon Eric, 8, 12, 17, 18, 115
Knapp-Fisher, Bishop E. G., 8, 12, 17, 115
Knox, Mgr. Ronald, 28
Kyrie, 114

Laity, 11, 13, 17, 18
Lambeth Appeal (1920), 97
— Conference (1920), 105; (1968), 21, 25, 118, 120–22
— Consultative Body, 120, 122
— Quadrilateral, 85, 88, 102
Lanne, Fr. E., 64, 66, 67
Laud, Archbishop William, 85
Lausanne, 27
Law, 11, 69, 70
Lectionary, Agreed, 93, 94, 111
Lee, F. G., 26
Leo XIII, Pope, 27, 29
Leuba, Prof., 63
Liberty, *see* Freedom

Liturgical Renewal, 10, 30–31, 110, 122
— Texts, Common, 13, 22, 82, 93, 94, 111, 116, 122
— Uniformity, 66
Liturgy, 2, 4, 11, 69, 70, 71, 72, 77, 78, 82, 83, 87, 89, 90, 93, 95, 104, 108, 110, 116, 121
Lord's Prayer, 114
Love, 11
Low Church, 76, 77
Lutheran(s), 48, 71, 92
Lutheran World Federation, 15
Lyons, 64

Magisterium, 16, 52, 85
Magnificat, 114
Malta, 23ff., 84, 93, 101, 107, 114, 116
— Report, 13, 23, 25, 107ff., 115, 116, 118, 120
Manning, Cardinal, 27
Marriage, 59, 111, 117
—, Joint Commission on, 13, 22, 25, 83, 92, 111, 120
Marriages, Mixed, 43, 44, 59, 83, 92, 93, 94, 111, 117
Mary, the Blessed Virgin, *and* Mariology, 11, 16, 22, 24, 43, 48, 49, 54, 56, 57, 67, 82, 83, 93, 94, 96, 102, 113, 121
Matthew, St., 70
McAdoo, Bishop H. R., 14, 20, 22, 23, 84ff., 115
Mediatrix, 49
Merit, 50, 55
Meyer, Dr. Harding, 15, 23
Ministry, 17, 23, 24, 53, 86, 96, 99, 102, 112, 113, 117, 122
Mission(s), 11, 38, 53, 62, 63, 92, 93, 94, 108, 111, 117, 121
Modernist Movement, 29, 30
Moeller, Fr. Charles, 68
Mollegen, Prof. A. T., 14, 115
Monastic Orders, *see* Religious Orders
Monothelitism, 49

Montreal, 52
Moorman, Bishop, J. R. H., 7, 10, 12, 17, 20, 74ff., 91, 115
Moral Questions, 21, 82, 83, 112, 113, 117, 121
More, P. E., 88
Mount St. Joseph, Mosta, 23

Nestorius, 67
New Christian, 98
New Testament, 61, 62, 63, 65, 96, 97, 98; Authority of, 15
Nicaea, First Council of, 47, 80
Nicene Creed, 47, 66, 89, 108, 114, 121
Novak, Michael, 80
Novatian Church, 65
Nunc Dimittis, 114

Old Catholic Churches, 20, 87, 96, 97
Old Testament, 60, 61, 93, 94
Original Sin, 42
Orthodox Churches, 19, 51, 53, 56, 71, 78, 79, 82, 90, 94, 95, 96, 98, 105

Pacifism, 83
Papacy *and* Papal Primacy, 17, 18, 19, 20, 22, 40, 43, 53, 54, 93, 94, 95, 96, 98, 102, 105, 113, 117, 121
Paschal Question, 64, 65
Pastoral Problems, 110
Patriarchates, 95
Patrick, Simon, 43
Paul VI, Pope, 1ff., 5, 6, 7, 13, 21, 24, 25, 26, 36, 72, 73, 77, 78, 80, 84, 87, 91, 93, 94, 102, 105, 107, 108, 114, 116, 120; Common Declaration of with Archbishop of Canterbury, 1ff., 6, 26, 84, 87, 92, 94, 102, 108, 114, 120
—, St., 1, 2, 3, 23, 26, 33, 61, 62, 63, 68, 69, 70, 73, 78, 80, 114
Pelagianism, 48

Penance, 54, 55, 56
Pentecost, 62
Permanent Joint Commission, Anglican/Roman Catholic (*later* Anglican/Roman Catholic International Commission), 25, 113, 118, 120, 122
Peter, St., 19, 20, 54, 61, 62, 63, 66, 70, 73, 86
Philippians, Epistle to the, 1, 2, 3, 26, 114
Philippou, A. J., 94
Pius IV, Pope, 42
— XI, Pope, 2, 7, 29
— XII, Pope, 28, 29, 43
Pluralism, 72, 78, 91
Polycarp, St., 65
Preachers, exchange of, 93, 94, 110, 121
Presence of Christ in the Eucharist, 58, 77
Priesthood, 58, 59, 77, 96, 98, 112, 117, 122
—, Universal, 11
Priests, 17
Pronouncements, Joint, 92, 93, 94, 105, 111, 117, 122
Protestant(s), 19, 51, 53, 58, 98, 105
Psalter, 114
Purdy, Canon W. A., 7, 9, 22, 23, 115
Purgatory, 42, 56

Ramsey, Archbishop Michael, *see* Canterbury
Reason, 85
Redemption, 49, 57, 61, 86
Reformation, 16, 24, 40, 41, 42, 45, 50, 52, 77
Reformed Churches, 10
Reformers, 16, 48
Relics, 43
Religious Orders, 77, 110, 117
Revelation, 23, 45, 51, 52, 102, 109

Richards, Fr. Michael, 10, 11, 12, 17, 22, 115
Rite, 72, 95, 96
Roman Empire, 63
Romans, Epistle to the, 62, 70
Rome, 1, 3, 5, 6, 19, 26, 64, 66, 68, 71, 73, 74
Root, Prof. H. E., 8, 12, 17, 21, 22, 74ff., 91, 115

Sacrament(s), 16, 18, 19, 23, 41, 42, 49, 54, 57, 58, 70, 72, 77, 78, 86, 87, 89, 96, 97, 98, 104, 105
Sadducees, 70
Salvation, 47, 48, 49, 50, 61, 70, 86
Samaria, 68
Sanctification, 49, 55
Sanctus, 114
Sanderson, R., 89
Sardica, Council of, 18
Satisfaction, 55, 56
Satterthwaite, Canon J. R., 7, 8, 115
Schillebeeckx, Fr. E., 80, 91
Schism(s), 17, 19, 21, 68, 69, 73
Schmemann, Fr. A., 95
Scripture(s) (Bible), 2, 4, 11, 12, 13, 15, 16, 22, 28–30, 33, 34, 40, 41, 43, 45, 46, 51, 52, 61, 65, 69, 77, 79, 85, 88, 90, 102, 108, 109, 121, 122
Shepherd, Dr. Massey H., Jnr., 8, 12, 19, 115
Sherlock, William, 43
Simon, Bishop W. G. H., 8, 12, 13, 15, 23, 115
Siricius, Pope, 66
Sixtus III, Pope, 68
Social Movement, 31–2
Socrates, 65
Soysa, Bishop C. H. W. de, 8, 115
Stephen, St., 63
Sursum Corda, 114
Surtees Society, 30
Syria, 68

Tablet, The, 25
Talbot, Mgr. G., 27
Tavard, Fr. George, 9, 12, 15,
    115
Taylor, Jeremy, 88
Te Deum, 114
Temple, Archbishop William,
    see Canterbury
Theological Education, 13, 92,
    93, 94, 110, 118, 121
Thirty-nine Articles, 88
Torah, 69, 70
Tradition(s), 2, 3, 4, 11, 12, 16,
    33, 38, 43, 45, 46, 51, 52, 65,
    68, 85, 87, 88, 102, 103, 108,
    109, 120, 121
Transjordania, 68
Transubstantiation, 42, 58
Trent, Council of, 40, 41, 42, 43,
    44
Trinity, 61, 66
Twelve Apostles, 19, 62, 63

Undivided Church, 17
Union Review, 26
Union Schemes, 10, 122
Uniqueness of the Church, 11,
    18
United Bible Societies, 34, 122
— States Roman Catholic
    Bishops' Commission for
    relations with Protestant
    Episcopal Church, 9
Utrecht, 87, 96

Vatican, 27, 116; Holy Office of,
    26, 27; Secretariat for
    Promoting Christian Unity
    of, 7, 9, 72, 113, 116, 117,
    118
— Council, First, 40, 93
— —, Second, 5, 15, 20, 21, 28,
    30, 31, 32, 33, 34, 35, 36, 51,
    53, 54, 57, 60, 70, 71, 72, 77,
    78, 80, 81, 83, 90, 91, 94, 96,
    98, 99, 102, 105, 109, 117;
    Anglican Observer(s) at, 5,

8; Documents of : On the
    Bishops' Pastoral Office
    (*Christus Dominus*), 71, 72;
    On the Church (*Lumen
    Gentium*), 31, 32, 33, 34, 36,
    49, 51, 53, 57, 60, 61, 62, 71,
    98, 99, 102; On the
    Church's Missionary
    Activity (*Ad Gentes*), 71,
    72; On the Church in the
    Modern World (*Gaudium
    et Spes*), 34, 35, 109; On
    Divine Revelation (*Dei
    Verbum*), 30, 33, 34, 51, 52,
    103, 122; On Eastern
    Catholic Churches
    (*Orientalium Ecclesiarum*),
    94, 95; On Ecumenism
    (*Unitatis Redintegratio*), 5,
    20, 28, 33, 35, 71, 72, 73, 78,
    79, 90, 92, 99, 103, 104, 108,
    109, 110, 117, 119; On
    Religious Freedom
    (*Dignitatis Humanae*), 92;
    On the Sacred Liturgy
    (*Sacrosanctum Concilium*),
    31, 71
Verdier, Cardinal, 32
Verghese, Fr. Paul, 10
Victor I, Pope, 64
Vincent of Lérins, St., 85, 87

Willebrands, Bishop J. G. M.,
    7, 9, 10, 12, 16, 20, 26ff.,
    60ff., 91, 115, 119
Windsor, 25
Witness, 13, 40, 111, 112, 122
Word of God, 12, 15, 16, 17, 18,
    45, 47, 49, 61, 70, 86, 102
World Council of Churches 52;
    Amsterdam Assembly of,
    28; Observer from, 7, 10,
    15, 23
Worship, Common, 93, 94, 103,
    104, 110, 121

York, 76